LOS ANGELES
Street Food

LOS ANGELES
Street Food

· A HISTORY FROM TAMALEROS TO TACO TRUCKS ·

FARLEY ELLIOTT

Published by American Palate
A Division of The History Press
Charleston, SC 29403
www.historypress.net

Copyright © 2015 by Farley Elliott
All rights reserved

First published 2015

Manufactured in the United States

ISBN 978.1.62619.991.0

Library of Congress Control Number: 2015940377

Dedicated to the tireless men and women who get up early and stay up late to make sure this golden city of ours remains well fed.
And to Kelsi Copeland, who is the great passion and architect of my life. This book has as much of her hard work in it as mine.

Contents

CONTENTS

Foreword

For more than 150 years, Los Angeles has been a street food capital, going back to the tamale wagons that were documented as early as the 1870s, although they may have been around even longer according to *Taco USA* author Gustavo Arellano. The tradition continued on L.A.'s first street, Olvera Street, in 1934 with El Cielito Lindo and the innovation of the catering truck by L.A.'s Mexican community, repackaged by chef Roy Choi's Kogi BBQ truck—but that's only part of the story.

Today in Los Angeles, there have never been more avenues to explore for street food, whether it be a food truck, street stand, taqueria, restaurant, underground restaurant in a private home or a market stall. That's not because of the growing street food craze all over the United States but because we've slowly revealed the layers of cuisine that have existed all along, hidden in cultural enclaves. To even a dedicated explorer such as myself, the exposed underbelly of L.A.'s itinerant dining scene has only revealed a call for a deeper journey into still undiscovered street food gems that await. Yes, it's the urban sprawl, and it's the ever-changing patterns of immigration, but really it's our lifestyle—Angelenos love street food.

From the Mexico City–style al pastor and Jaliscan tacos de fritanga vendors in South Central Los Angeles to the Capulhuac barbacoa specialists in Jefferson Park to the Guatemalan tamal and tostada vendors in MacArthur Park—and even at the fancy graphic-wrapped and Twitterized food trucks on the Miracle Mile—street food is what feeds us. Food trucks were popular in Los Angeles first, when Mexican American vendors started to buy catering trucks to satisfy the cravings of construction workers and ESL students and then took to parking them just about anyplace where Latinos gathered. This spread throughout the United States in small waves, and then came chef Roy Choi's Kogi.

The Kogi truck ushered in a new worldwide movement of food trucks with all roads leading back to Los Angeles, where the growing audience not only embraced the shiny, international foods offered and the chef-driven trucks but also looked back to the classics like Mariscos Jalisco, Tacos Leo and Tacos Los Güichos. The climate was never better for Ensenada native Ricky Piña of Ricky's Fish Tacos to get his own truck. Fast forward a few years from there to the ultimate Los Angeles truck, Guerrilla Tacos, a concept by Mexican American chef Wes Avila, who has taken the Los Angeles taco to new heights.

Simply put, L.A. has the best street food scene, including Mexican, Guatemalan, Salvadoran, food trucks and the various Asian cuisines that Los Angeles does so well: Chinese, Korean and Thai. Though the Asian restaurateurs prefer brick-and-mortar locations, many still rely on street food menus, and for everything else there are the 626 Night Markets, which have brought some of those great Asian dishes back down to our level: the street. We've led the way from the tamale wagons to taco trucks to the commercial trucks to the growing regional specialists that sprinkle their spices all over the Los Angeles landscape. It's the greatest street food show in the country, and we've still yet to discover it.

—BILL ESPARZA

Los Angeles's premier street food writer and chronicler of all things Mexican food

Acknowledgements

This book is a group effort, composed of more people than can ever fully be named here. A few notables, though:

Noam Bleiweiss
Brett Morris
Paul Bartunek
Clay Larsen
Liezl Estipona
Julia Reed
Jakob N. Layman
Amy Scattergood
Matt Kang
Bill Esparza
Tony Chen
Serious Eats
LA Weekly
Eater
Republique
Dinosaur Coffee
Sqirl

Introduction

First and foremost, this book is meant to be a tool, so use it as you see fit. Throw it in your glove box or tear pages out and hand them to friends in their moments of street food need. Keep it in a glass case behind a sign that says, "Break only in case of taco emergency." It's yours to enjoy and destroy. After all, what good is a book that covers tacos, tamales, bacon-wrapped hot dogs, Taiwanese grilled meat skewers and ice cream sandwiches if it can't stand to get a little messy?

In lots of ways, it is messiness that defines Los Angeles. We don't give people directions based on addresses or, as in New York, intersections. We talk in imprecise travel times and general compass navigations, using landmarks to guide us through neighborhoods that change drastically by the block. It's a messy town, full of cars and people and smog, with no cleanly defined center to speak of.

But it is in that messiness that we Angelenos thrive. Many of our street vendors are illegal and our immigrants undocumented, but beneath that legal murk, there is a simmering subculture that truly warms this city. It always has been, and always will be, a place for people escaping something else.

We are the second-largest Mexican city in the world by population. There are more Koreans here than anywhere else on the planet, outside of Korea itself. Los Angeles is the permanent home for nearly half a million Chinese and roughly as many Armenians. We have Guatemalans, Iranians, Indians, Japanese and Brits, all fitting together in a loose jumble covering almost five thousand square miles. That's awesome.

Shrimp tacos dorados from the Mariscos Jalisco truck. *Paul Bartunek.*

And because of this diversity, because we have chosen to build out instead of up, Los Angeles has come be known as a world-class street food city. We have the space for it, the background for it and the hunger for it, and more and more the rest of the world is beginning to see the truth. You can sample cuisines from all across the globe just by spending an afternoon in L.A. and eat better on the streets than in most restaurants across America.

This book helps to define where Los Angeles is, right now, as a street food city. It's about where the city has come from and where it stands now, on the verge of major street food regulation reform. It's about the types of street food you can enjoy here, from carts and tables to taco trucks and gourmet catering outfits, with farmers' markets and food festivals thrown in for good measure.

This book is not exhaustive, it's not complete and it doesn't tell the whole story because it can't. Street food doesn't work like that. It's too messy.

Grab a plate and get your hands dirty.

Part 1

THE HISTORY AND POLITICS OF STREET FOOD

Chapter 1
The Ever-Changing Nature of L.A.'s Street Food Scene

O nce you've lived in Los Angeles long enough, you start to take street food for granted. Maybe you don't eat it often, and so the passing blur of hot dog carts and gourmet food trucks seems to blend in with the rest of the city as a sort of constant grayscale. Or maybe you eat at taco trucks or from tamale carts all the time, either as a necessary replacement for a

El Matador in East Hollywood. *Jakob N. Layman.*

home-cooked meal or simply because it's delicious, and it's become entirely ingrained in your ongoing routine. In either case, the notion of street food acts as a constant, without much thought to where it came from or where it's going.

But the truth is, street food is not a constant. It's not static and certainly hasn't always been an accepted part of how Los Angeles eats. Street food is amorphous in every way possible: as a topic of conversation, as an ever-changing destination, as a cultural history. It is always moving and adapting, just as it has since its introduction to L.A. roughly 150 years ago, and it tends to slip through our fingers just at the moment we think we've got a handle on it.

Chapter 2
A Historically Mexican Tradition

The first street food vendors in Los Angeles didn't rise to prominence until the latter half of the nineteenth century, following a rush of outside attention that hit the city in the wake of California's successful bid to become the thirty-first state in the union in September 1850. Until then, California as a whole was stuck in a bit of a legal and social holding pattern, particularly during and immediately following the Mexican-American War, which ran from 1846 to 1848.

When the Treaty of Guadalupe Hidalgo ended all the fighting in 1848, the Mexican government was forced to hand over full authoritative control for what at the time was known as Alta California, a massive swath of land that hugged the coast from present-day Sonoma on down and ran east into Nevada and beyond. Within two years, California was born.

At the time, however, Los Angeles was not the powerhouse city that it is now. San Francisco was long seen as the coastal jewel of California, having experienced earlier successes with migration westward and all the money that came from the gold rush. Much of Southern California was, instead, a haven for agriculture—particularly citrus, which grew in abundance but was seen as a luxury elsewhere.

For Los Angeles, the cascading arrival of the gold rush, the rise of the transcontinental railroad and the newly achieved statehood couldn't have come at a better time. By the time the Southern Pacific railroad route fully linked Los Angeles to all points east in 1876, the medium-sized agricultural center was beginning to truly come to life. And so, too, were the first signs of street food.

One of the first known drawings of Los Angeles, between 1847 and 1849. *William Rich Hutton, courtesy USC digital library.*

Tamale men from Mexico and Chinese immigrants working pushcarts were the first to arrive in any real meaningful way. As Gustavo Arellano says in his seminal look at the movement of Mexican food into America, *Taco USA*: "The origins of the city's tamale sellers are murky, although newspaper accounts place them as far back as the 1870s." Within a decade, men selling the handmade masa treats were commonplace around what is now downtown Los Angeles, arriving early to stake out spots or pushing their two-wheeled carts through El Pueblo de Los Angeles.

Early efforts at street food regulation came swiftly. By the 1890s, there were city government–sanctioned attempts to either severely limit or curb these tamaleros altogether, by restricting either their movement or their

window for being able to sell. Most efforts to crack down on the street vendors failed miserably because then, as now, Mexican street food simply proved too popular.

By the turn of the century, the city had agreed instead to force tamale cart owners to pay for operating licenses as a way to weed them out, but it only helped to de-stigmatize the market for tamales without slowing it down. Arellano points in his book to a *Los Angeles Times* article from the era that notes that arriving strangers often "remark[ed] at the presence of so many outdoor restaurants," though nearby brick-and-mortar restaurants remained none too happy.

Much of this early action was clustered in and around downtown, due in large part to the expansive nature of Los Angeles even then. Vendors couldn't simply transport themselves across town to other small neighborhoods, so the density of vendors in and around El Pueblo started to become a problem. An attempt to outlaw tamale carts altogether in the early 1900s failed, but within several years, the explosive growth of the city and the slow rise of the automobile had chipped away at some of that downtown dominance.

By the mid-1920s, L.A.'s street food landscape had at once exploded (thanks to the influx of Mexican immigrants into the half-century-old state) and dissipated, with more vendors finding easier access to customers across a wider swath of the city. These new street food operators brought with them more than just the tamale, and by the 1930s, tacos were all the rage in Los Angeles.

Chapter 3
Chinese Street Vendors

At the same time historically, Los Angeles's fluctuating Chinese population was faring much, much worse. In her book *Fit to Be Citizens*, author Natalia Molina outlines the rough path that L.A.'s Chinese, many brought to America during the railroad boom, faced in becoming an accepted part of city society. Easily marginalized, Chinese immigrants were held to certain slums and ghettoized areas near the busy downtown, unable to move to quieter, more sanitary property. The unhealthy results then further propagated themselves, and by the 1870s, several large-scale attacks on Chinese homes and businesses had dropped the ethnic population to just a few hundred.

The turn of the century didn't help matters much, as a few waves of disease spread throughout Los Angeles, mostly (either correctly, thanks to the squalid conditions they were forced to live in, or incorrectly and owing to some overt racism) attributed to the Chinese contingent. Still, throughout it all, enterprising Chinese vendors had begun to make a name for themselves, mostly as pushcart operators selling fresh produce and small snacks.

By 1910, in concurrence with the ongoing attempts to regulate tamale carts and other Mexican street foods, the City of Los Angeles enacted strict regulations on outdoor vending. One of the unofficial stipulations of the new efforts was segregation between white and non-white vendors, wherein whites were given access to downtown's newer, city-subsidized marketplaces. (The Grand Central Market, which was founded in 1917 and still stands today, was not far off.)

Chinese, on the other hand, were forced to vend on the move, selling in the streets and by knocking on doors, with the city undermining their efforts at

Economy Meats at Grand Central Market in 1940. *Courtesy Grand Central Market.*

every turn. "There remains little doubt," says Molina in her book, "that public health officials considered Chinese street vendors unsanitary and unscrupulous. They warned the public not to purchase any goods from them."

Despite facing government-sanctioned monopolizing by white vendors in order to undercut prices by sometimes as much as 50 percent, as well as near-constant harassment by regulators and police, Chinese street vendors continued to serve the neighborhoods that relied on them. It wasn't really until the middle of the 1920s, when the political decision to revitalize the historic Pueblo downtown by creating what is today Olvera Street came to pass, that much of the Chinese street vending culture disappeared.

The nearby Chinatown was forced to move and consolidate farther away from the designed historical site, and many of the carts faded away. By the time Olvera Street opened in 1930, just two years before the 1932 Olympics held in Los Angeles, much of the street vending in the area had been run off completely so as not to compete with the Americanized sit-down Mexican restaurants in the area. Similar stories befell Japanese immigrant farmers and vendors at the time, until eventually the only group that held on to its love of street food was Latin Americans.

Chapter 4
Competition Arrives

By 1917, downtown's Grand Central Market had arrived, giving the booming L.A. population a consolidated place to shop and eat (though at the expense of ethnic minority vendors elsewhere in the city). Seventeen years later, the Original Farmers Market opened far across the city at

A Grand Central Market vendor in 1940. *Courtesy Grand Central Market.*

the intersection of what are today Third and Fairfax. In both cases, stalls were erected to house individual vendors, completely forgoing the need for mobilization. Very quickly, the dynamics of street food shifted, as customers began to cluster at markets and certain vendor points to seek out the best food rather than waiting for someone to roll past their front doors with a meal on a cart.

The skyrocketing expansion of urban manufacturing in and around Los Angeles, brought on by easy access to the ports in the South Bay and rail lines connecting downtown, led to another small wave of street food vending in the early 1940s. Sandwich makers and hot dog salesmen began to buy up fully mobile trailers, attaching them to cars and parking them near aerospace companies and automotive manufacturers. The idea of sneaking out of the plant in time to grab a quick bite to eat under the open sky was appealing and had become commonplace by the 1940s.

Less than ten years later, Southern California would be rocked by the widespread advent of fast food, with its speedy service and drive-through windows. Given the appealing option to enjoy reasonable-quality food at an affordable price point while not even getting out of the car, many Southern California residents chose to spend their money on burgeoning chains like McDonald's and Glen Bell's Taco-Tia, which became today's Taco Bell. What's worse, these fast-food chains often co-opted the same meals that had previously been considered street food staples, homogenizing and commodifying them until they looked a far sight from the original product. Hot dogs and tacos, long street food staples, were particularly hard hit.

A parking lot hot dog truck parks outside of an aerospace company in 1940. *Courtesy Ansel Adams, LAPL.*

27

The silver lining to all of this, surprisingly, comes from Taco Bell itself, which Arellano argues in his book used co-opted recipes from a San Bernardino Mexican restaurant to form the hard-shelled foundation of its growing taco empire. Though the growth of the fast-food industry came in many ways at the expense of (particularly Mexican) street food, Taco Bell's nationwide roll out did help to promote at least a version of Mexican food. It introduced small-town America to the taco, the burrito or simple rice and beans, albeit in a very bastardized form.

Fifty years later, chefs like Roy Choi would use that familiarity to draw people in before playing on a much bigger concept: that street tacos can be as engaging and as important as anything served up inside of a high-end restaurant.

During the fast-food boom and through the 1960s and '70s, street food certainly didn't disappear in Los Angeles, but it did largely move back to its cultural center. By letting Americans appropriate their cuisine into something altogether unfamiliar, Mexican and Central American vendors in particular were able to hold on to the recipes that had earned them recognition in the first place and keep those customers who could tell the difference in the process.

Chapter 5
L.A.'s Modern Influx

The most recent wave of street food dominance in Los Angeles actually began close to forty years ago, thanks to an overwhelming pilgrimage of Central American and Mexican immigrants escaping issues in their home countries. Many arrived illegally and, finding themselves unable to work aboveboard jobs, turned to street vending as a way to make ends meet. In short order, city regulators and the police once again turned on the vendors as they had eighty or one hundred years before, attempting to drive them off through a war of outright aggression.

Researcher Fazila Bhimji chronicled many of these issues in her anthropological work *Struggles, Urban Citizenship, and Belongings*, laying out a timeline of harassment, particularly against female street vendors during these years. Over one nine-month period in 1987 alone, the paper notes, nearly 250 vendors were outright convicted of crimes for selling food on the street, with nearly 30 percent spending time in jail as a result.

By 1994, protests over the treatment of street vendors had hit city hall, which responded by having officers issue over eight hundred tickets to vendors in and around MacArthur Park over the course of only a few weeks. The planned crackdown backfired, with the local media and neighborhood consumers coming together to push for relaxed enforcement in the face of a lack of much meaningful regulation from the city. Street food, as always, belonged to the people, and those people would never let it disappear.

Some attempts at balanced regulation measures did come to pass during this time and have gone on to help stitch together the patchwork

A downtown street hot dog vendor in 1996. *Courtesy Anthony Friedkin, LAPL.*

of laws and oversight that is meant to guide today's street food vendors. Commissary kitchens were established that would, in effect, allow vendors to prep food on site before moving to the streets to sell, though not on any public land like in parks or on sidewalks. Instead, vendors must not only work within the confines of (and pay rent to) a nearby commissary, but they must also pass routine paid health inspections, lease a cart for their work and pay for storage rights on all of their equipment. The result, particularly for the growing influx of undocumented immigrants from nations like El Salvador and Guatemala, was a rift between hardworking vendors who could afford to play by the rules and unlicensed operators who enjoyed all of the benefits of street food vending but eschewed the pricey overhead.

By the mid-2000s, Los Angeles's street food scene was again ready for a change. Staid laws hadn't slowed down its growth, and more and more consumers were starting to become conscious of the food they ate and where it came from. Intrepid writers and eaters began to explore the city's street food meccas in South L.A. and Boyle Heights, particularly where trucks and tables congregated. Breed Street in Boyle Heights became ground zero for late-night Mexican street food parties, even garnering a review of sorts by

Burmese khao soi from an illegal vendor in Monterey Park. *Clay Larsen.*

LA Weekly writer Jonathan Gold in 2009, near the end of its run. Growing attention on the Breed Street vendors ultimately forced them to disperse, following a few high-profile crackdowns by the city.

The city's heightened awareness of street food, coupled with a changing national attitude toward the way we think about where our meals come from, couldn't have come at a better time. By late 2008 and early 2009, shifting markets had allowed a new kind of quality-conscious street food to emerge: the gourmet food truck.

Chapter 6
The Gourmet Street Food Revolution

E very good idea needs a strong-willed person to see it through, and in the case of L.A.'s (and largely, the nation's) street food revolution, that man is Roy Choi. The longtime restaurant chef with an upscale pedigree is, more than anyone, credited with entirely revamping the street food industry.

The Kogi BBQ truck. *Paul Bartunek.*

Choi's first burst of fame came by way of Kogi BBQ, a dingy, roaming white food truck covered in skate apparel stickers. After spending years working in hotel kitchens and on stuffy restaurant lines, Choi and his partners emerged in late 2008 with the idea of Kogi BBQ, a Korean fusion experience that marries two of the biggest demographics in Los Angeles. Quesadillas would get stuffed with kimchi, tacos filled with a Korean-spiced short rib. Definitely not authentic, but definitely delicious.

"Authenticity lies in tradition and technique and culture," Choi, who has become something of a street food philosopher after all these years, says now. "We must remember that they are all created by people and therefore can change. Nostalgia is in the mind."

Using the genre-busting menu as a gateway, Choi and the Kogi team slung tacos on the streets of Hollywood for weeks, getting tourists, bouncers and locals to try the unique menu, all while using Twitter as a way to draw in and engage with a wider audience. Soon, customers began arriving in droves, pointed to a particular location by the social media team behind Kogi BBQ.

It could be Compton one night, Mid-City another and Santa Monica the day after that. Kogi not only revamped the idea of what late-night food—and fusion food, in particular—could be, but it also changed the way that people thought about Los Angeles geographically. People from upscale neighborhoods would drive to some of the poorest sections of the city just to stand in line for a short rib taco. In that first year, Choi and his team fed everyone and anyone who was willing to eat.

"Food trucks can go anywhere, from Bel Air to Belmont now," says Choi. "And Kogi changed that, straight up."

He's right. Kogi changed a lot of things about Los Angeles street food, forever. By the end of 2009, dozens of food trucks had emerged in L.A., some as direct competitors (and bold rip-offs) of Kogi itself, others with their own concepts and determined chefs. Operators like the Grilled Cheese Truck were early adopters of the gourmet street food lifestyle, as were Dogtown Dogs and other well-known trucks that still run on the streets today.

By 2010, the market was already beginning to look flooded. *The Great Food Truck Race* premiered on the Food Network in August of that year, with local burger makers Grill 'Em All taking home top prize (they've since moved into a brick-and-mortar restaurant space). But on the ground, longtime vendors were competing for space and customers with newer, shinier trucks—and oftentimes a lot of financial backing.

Longtime local street food operations (mostly the staple corner taco truck, operating from a simple lonchero) generally managed to stay afloat

A trio of tacos from the Kogi BBQ truck. *Paul Bartunek.*

during this tumultuous time. Despite the initial pressure to outperform the competition, gourmet food trucks and local street vendors formed a mostly symbiotic relationship, with the increased overall presence of street food in the wider media helping to propel both sides to successes not seen before, while de-stigmatizing the entire street food culture in the process.

In the years since the early food truck boom, many gourmet operators have moved into brick-and-mortar restaurants (or several, as is the case with the Komodo truck, which still has a street presence as well). Others have been bought out or franchised, but many of the higher-end new wave of trucks have simply ceased operation altogether. Street food vending was never for the faint of heart, as plenty of chefs, owners and quick-money businessmen soon found out.

Today's gourmet food truck scene is a far cry from the market in 2010 or 2011. Vendors can't rely on social media exclusively as a customer driver, so they've expanded into routine, planned stops at locations with lots of customers or toward private catering gigs. Instead of chasing a truck from one end of the city to the other, curious diners now either rely on their favorite trucks to stick to a predetermined schedule that matches their own lifestyles or go out of their way to seek out trucks at large events or curated evenings.

Inside the Grilled Cheese Truck. *Elizabeth Daniels.*

As for the true street food vendors—the bacon-wrapped hot dog sellers, the champurrado pourers, the lonchero drivers—as a whole, they haven't gone anywhere. Buoyed by increased consumer comfort with street food, once again these authentic operators are moving to the forefront of the Los Angeles dining scene. Maybe they're being heralded at one of the many food festivals in town or asked to move into a permanent or semi-permanent space inside of a food hall.

Chapter 7
The Politics of Street Food

There are still issues of policing that come with such a heightened presence, however. Much of Los Angeles's street vending operations are still wholly illegal, operating without permits on public property and with the very real fear that at any moment their livelihood could be thrown in the back of a trash truck.

Burmese food from an illegal backyard vendor in Monterey Park. *Clay Larsen.*

Los Angeles's vending laws are nearly as archaic toward street food today as they were one hundred years ago, but the tides are changing. An influx of like-minded city hall officials has aimed to bring clarity to the situation, enabling street vendors to sell their wares in peace, so long as they follow the proper protocols. For street food–heavy neighborhoods like Boyle Heights, that's a boon not only to the economy but also to the local population that has either come to rely on the extra income earned from a second shift working a grill or by being the customer who needs to eat well—and cheap—during off hours.

There also exists very little homogeny within the overall landscape of Los Angeles when it comes to street food regulation. Cities-within-cities like Beverly Hills can often shape their street food policy independently of the larger organism, which in years past led to plenty of struggle and confusion. There were local

Taiwanese meat skewers at an Asian night market in Los Angeles. *Noam Bleiweiss.*

ordinances passed, town hall meetings that erupted into shouting matches and often disproportionate responses by police when cracking down on illegal or unlicensed street food vendors. To say nothing of the murky legal grounds of unincorporated parts of the county, where fewer regulations led to a proliferation of street food with little or no accountability.

But in truth, there has always been some sense of politicking and gerrymandering to the street food process in Los Angeles, even without county health and safety regulations. For decades, permit and parking restrictions have worked to keep the perceived riff raff out of particular residential neighborhoods or corralled them into workable commercial clusters. As a result, much of the concentration of street food still happens outside the major urban core of Los Angeles. The taco carts and fruit vendors seen from downtown to Santa Monica are but a fraction of the larger scene, which thrives largely unchecked in areas like Boyle Heights, the northeast Valley and South L.A. These have become street food meccas for those willing to seek such things out, but their inability to safely and legitimately vend closer to the city's core speaks volumes about the way these vendors are seen by many of those in charge.

And still, after more than 150 years, there has never been a better time to be serving, eating and learning about Los Angeles's street food culture. Licensed and unlicensed vendors share common space across the city, earning catering gigs and setting up shop in front of weekday business parks. Street food festivals are more popular than ever, serving thousands who come to see what all the fuss is about.

Through waves of popularity and potential interlopers, through years of harsh citywide enforcement and foggy regulations, street food remains an indelible part of this city. It is important both as a cultural indicator and as a survival tool, feeding thousands every night.

It also happens to be delicious.

Part 11

THE STREET FOOD LANDSCAPE IN LOS ANGELES TODAY

Chapter 8
The Many Types of Street Food

There are many different types of street food experiences possible in Los Angeles, from upscale dinners that pair perfectly with an outdoor film screening to late-night, post-drinking dalliances with low-grade hot dogs cooked over a retrofitted shopping cart. Each is unique in its own way and offers a particular type of dining experience.

Of course, location is always a factor, particularly in sprawling Los Angeles. Unlike the early days of the boom, a roaming gourmet food truck is only as worthwhile as its proximity to you now. Similarly, it's entirely possible that the city's undisputed street food king of shrimp tacos will be an hour's drive away from you, making it likely to lose some of its luster.

What that means is that more often than not, the best street food experiences you can have in Los Angeles are specific to you in the moment that your hunger strikes. Where are you? What are you craving? How much money do you have in your pocket? What time is it, and how much time do you have to spend? Answering these questions should help to point you in a given direction, whether it's that new nighttime taco truck that just started parking around the corner or the daytime Guatemalan vendors begging to be sought out in MacArthur Park.

You should also try to very honestly assess your own comfort levels and those of anyone who might be joining you on your dining adventure. Your level of comfort with the format and type of street food you choose to eat is entirely up to you. If you aren't entirely enticed by the idea of late-night

Street vendors prepare tortillas by hand. *Paul Bartunek.*

cow brain tacos, that's OK—there's probably a different street food dinner experience near you that might be more up your alley.

So, look around you. Ask a local. Consult a restaurant app or thumb through the pages of a guidebook like this one. Street food is everywhere in Los Angeles, and it isn't even trying to hide. You just have to know what you're looking for.

Chapter 9
One-Off Vendors

One-off vendors are perhaps the most literal translation of street food available in Los Angeles. Unencumbered by trucks, deadlines, social media and investors and operating without the legal baggage that comes from a city with a defined street food regulation and enforcement plan, these intrepid solo operators are free to move about at whim, sell when they want to and make determinations about every level of their business.

The idea of the one-off vendor is also an ancient one, carried through for centuries from roving pushcarts carrying freshly killed fowl from door to door, on through to takeaway sandwich makers, big-city hot dog carts and Baltimore's dying arabbers, men who corral horse-drawn carriages full of fresh fruit through the poorest neighborhoods in town.

These single salesmen have done more than simply shape the way in which Los Angeles considers its street food—they defined the entire market in the first place. Today's tamale vendors work the same land their ancestors did more than a century ago. Back when there were men to shine shoes and boys to call out the day's headlines—always one man for one job—there were street food vendors selling a reasonably priced alternative to cooking something up at home.

Today's vendors still operate in much the same way. Often isolated, they work odd hours in order to catch maximum foot traffic leaving a bar or during a lunch rush at a busy office building. Lacking signage or a company name, these workers largely become homogenous. They all feel the same, and they all blend seamlessly into the greater fabric of what it means to eat in Los Angeles.

An ice cream vendor in Echo Park. *Farley Elliott.*

Forget taco trucks, gourmet food trucks and even fully built hot dog carts; Los Angeles's quiet, unassuming one-off vendors are the ones who will keep you fed when no one else can. There are no accolades for "best fruit vendor" or "best bacon-wrapped hot dog"; the reward is having been able to serve—and to make a little money in the process.

Bacon—Wrapped Hot Dog Vendors

Dirty Dogs. Danger Dogs. Heart Attack Dogs. Street Meat. Everyone has their personal favorite slang for L.A.'s most famous street food claim: the bacon-wrapped hot dog.

It all sounds so beguilingly simple: take low-quality hot dogs, wrap pieces of bacon around them, grill them until cooked completely through and serve them to anyone who'll eat them. But as it turns out, the politics and problems behind street food bacon dogs have been complicating matters for years.

First, to get this out of the way: bacon-wrapped hot dog vendors are illegal. Under the current legal network that governs such things in Los Angeles County, they are very, very illegal—but so is much of L.A.'s street food culture. Or, at the very least, illegal in the sense that they're unlicensed.

Upon first inspection of a bacon-wrapped hot dog vendor's rig, it's not hard to sympathize with the people whose job it is to tell the vendors that they potentially pose a health hazard. There is nothing remotely aboveboard going on with carts like these.

Usually, they are actual shopping carts, slightly retrofitted to house two small chafing dish fuel canisters inside the open shell of the cart itself, held up by a thin wire rack. Over that heat source goes a plain sheet pan, the kind available at any restaurant discount store or home baker's cupboard. The properly positioned fuel underneath heats the metal pan through so completely that it acts as a makeshift griddle, sizzling up hot dogs and caramelizing onions all night long. The rest of the cart is used for ingredient storage, maybe a boombox, and the wheels allow for an easy getaway if things get hairy.

Street vendors outside of a church in Echo Park. *Farley Elliott.*

From a health inspector's vantage point, though, the things that are missing are almost too numerous and important to count. A staging area to properly prep and hold supplies at refrigerated temperatures, sanitary wipes or clean kitchen towels and a thermometer to make sure the bacon is cooked to its required doneness. They don't call them danger dogs for nothin'.

Still, there are few things better and more readily available after a hard night of drinking than a bacon-wrapped hot dog. The smell is intoxicating and only seems to intensify as the night goes on. The sizzle of bacon fat and the slow griddling of a low-grade hot dog, combined with the earthy aroma of cooking onions and peppers—that is the smell of places like Hollywood Boulevard on many weekend nights. Top off the dog with a squirt each of ketchup and mayonnaise and a grilled jalapeño, all for five dollars or less, and you've got your hands on the real patron saint of Los Angeles street food.

As with all one-off vendors, timing, location and price will always be approximate. Hollywood Boulevard, particularly at night and more so on the weekends, will always be a readily available place to find your first (or next) bacon-wrapped hot dog. Popular entertainment venues that get out late also make for great places to hunt down a danger dog—Staples Center (on the south side at least, where it's a bit less touristy), Dodgers Stadium, music venues like the Echoplex in Echo Park, the Forum and many movie theaters.

For an all-day look at where these vendors tend to congregate, the best option is to head into any one of L.A.'s underserved neighborhoods. The fashion district downtown is known for always having at least one hot dog cart around, and it wouldn't take long to cruise down Central Avenue into South L.A. before one popped up. It's also a good idea to hit places like Elysian Park, which attracts families and thus street vendors.

The best option, really, is to just let the bacon-wrapped hot dog happen to you. Rather than trying to seek out the experience itself, go out and have the type of experience that would bring those vendors around. Enjoy a show, stay out late, explore an unfamiliar neighborhood. Just when you need it most, that's when you'll catch a waft of the familiar smell of cheap bacon being cooked in a sheet pan from inside a shopping cart nearby. And, strange as it may sound given the description, it'll be a very welcome smell.

THE STREET FOOD LANDSCAPE IN LOS ANGELES TODAY

TAMALE VENDORS

It is one of L.A.'s great shames that many of our city's tamale vendors still must work in the shadows, afraid of being harassed by police or sometimes even thrown in jail for selling the product they love. Men and women have been selling tamales in the city since its inception, and the fact that there is still no worthwhile legislation on the books to properly manage the process at a price that isn't astronomical is mind-boggling.

What's especially troubling is the seeming lack of understanding on the part of city officials when dealing in particular with the many tamaleros of Los Angeles. Tamales, unlike bacon-wrapped hot dogs, are by their definition a cooked food, often made with shredded meats, moles or options like warm beans, corn and cheese. The whole thing is wrapped and steamed to completion before it's even able to be sold. Otherwise, there's no tamal, just a raw piece of masa with some stuff inside.

And yet, tamale vendors must be stricken with the same fears as other unlicensed one-off operators.

The only real legal recourse, short of opening a full catering truck or small brick-and-mortar business, is to join a commissary kitchen. The process is not only arduous and occasionally unfriendly to the elderly, illegal immigrants and people for whom English is a second language (which makes up a disproportionate amount of all street vendors), but it's also vastly more expensive and time-consuming. In a market where most tamale vendors sell their products at one dollar apiece, it can seem almost impossible to pay commissary fees, health inspection fees and licensing fees and still have anything left over at the end of the day.

Which is why so many tamaleros simply take to the streets, affordably selling their product without fear of rising overhead costs or a steep learning curve. There won't ever be much money for a single individual operating in this game—$30 here, $100 there—but it's a worthwhile living on one's own terms.

You'll find these tamaleros, often selling their product on the sly from repurposed Igloo coolers or hidden away under blankets, wherever Mexican and Central Americans congregate. In high-density areas like South L.A., Boyle Heights and San Fernando, one-off vendors selling tamales wrapped in corn husks or banana leaves (the latter being a Southern Mexico/Central American phenomenon) are simply everywhere. They may be pushing carts full of tamales down side streets, yelling out to potential customers in their houses about the items for sale. You can find them on street corners, huddled up with a couple other vendors to form an ad hoc one-stop shop for anyone driving by. In parking lots, parks and playgrounds, you will find tamaleros selling their version of ten-thousand-year-old food.

In more ethnically diverse neighborhoods like Koreatown and Westlake, tamale vendors tend to cluster together in order to attract just enough attention to draw in customers without alerting the health department, the police or immigration.

One such battleground is MacArthur Park in Westlake, which has been cleaned up considerably over the years but can still be a little rough. Here, tamaleros work together to ward off local gangs looking to secure turf payment and alert one another when a crackdown is coming. Dozens of vendors of largely Mexican and Guatemalan heritage operate daily, alongside playing children, officeworkers on their lunch break and the occasional man selling fake IDs.

Pushing hardworking street vendors into areas like this works as a kind of measured standoff between authorities and sellers. No one wins, really, but the losses are pretty minimal overall. And until something can be done to update the way in which Los Angeles thinks about and treats its street food vendors, places like this is where they'll have to remain.

Fruit Carts

One of L.A.'s most colorful street food options is the fruit cart. Nearly as ubiquitous as the bacon-wrapped hot dog, but perhaps more visible thanks to its daytime presence, fruit cart vendors operate no-name carts and stands in front of office buildings, in parks and probably even outside of your local DMV, cutting fresh fruit to order for anyone who's interested in a quick snack.

All that color comes from the actual fruit on display, stacked inside of a glass enclosure atop the cart. Sliced pineapples, cut melons and bags of limes sit atop pounds of slowly melting ice, ensuring a sweet, cooling treat for the hot summer months. Add to that the shiny silver box of the cart itself, plus the rainbow-tinged umbrellas that act as calling cards and safety from the sun, and you've got a vibrant vending operation available on just about every street corner in the city.

Like almost every other popular L.A. street snack, the fruit cart finds its heritage in Mexico and Central America, largely. These simple one-man stands are relatively cheap for vendors and customers alike, rely on an abundance of fresh local fruit and can be replenished with ease, making them long a favorite in the larger cities to America's south.

Here in L.A., local regulations (in theory) force carts off public property and sidewalks, though that's exactly where you're most likely to find them. Besides the above locations, you'll find fruit carts in front of banks, on open street corners, near hospitals and even—curiously enough—right in front of grocery stores like the Whole Foods on the southeastern corner of Third Street and Fairfax Avenue (but only on weekends).

Their popularity and regularity owes largely to the product they sell. Rather than trying to get potentially wary customers to opt-in for a bacon-wrapped hot dog or tamales sold by the half dozen, fruit cart vendors need only rely on the freshness of their product and the sun, which has a way of baking off the asphalt and making the carts seem pretty tempting.

As for a menu of options—well, there isn't one. This is "what you see is what you get" territory, where the visible options are the only options on the table. That leads, in the best cases, to bit of cart customization—locals may well have their favorite nearby carts that sell exclusively the fruits they like and none that they don't.

Mixed bags of cut fruit are king here, so just step up and tell your friendly local fruit cart vendor exactly what you're after. Feel free to point as needed; it's part of the reason those colorful visual aides are there in the first place. In a flash, your fruits of choice are removed from the case, hacked up into manageable chunks and then dropped into a waiting clear plastic bag. You're given a plastic fork for easy use, and off you go!

That is, unless you want the true street fruit cart experience, which adds a load of spicy dried seasoning and a healthy squirt of lime to the bag. Tajin is the most popular flavoring, a Jalisco, Mexico–based blend that relies on dried ground chile peppers, plenty of salt and dehydrated lime juice. It's the same stuff they commonly add to micheladas, and it adds a bit of punch and flavor to your inexpensive fruit snack.

While it certainly is possible to grab a bag of fruit without a dash of the stuff, it's not recommended. Spicy, acidic bags of fresh fruit are a true institution within L.A.'s street food scene, and it's certainly an experience worth enjoying for yourself.

Chapter 10
Cart, Table and Stand Vendors

A small step up from the ad hoc operations of a typical one-off vendor, the folks who work carts, tables and stands across Los Angeles have actual equipment to use and often stay in one place for long stretches, occasionally becoming well-known in the process.

That's not to say there aren't nomadic carts and tables. At this level of street food vending, odds are high that this is just a second (or third) job for someone in a local family rather than a full-time source of income. So as needs and desires change, so too do the winds of street vending.

A popular late-night taco table, with nothing more than a cauldron of slowly simmering meats or a spinning spit of marinated pork, could exist for years in the same location before abruptly closing up forever, thanks to a land-use agreement gone bad or a personal family matter. There is often no brand for a cart like this, no media recognition coming, just years of weekly dedication to a craft that keeps people well fed.

On the other hand, there are examples like the Blue Corn Quesadilla Lady of Echo Park who exist as almost mythic cart vendors. Food writers and locals looking for a bite of something special might spend weeks trying to track down a particular cart or table before stumbling on it when least expected. Others, like the walk-up stand Yuca's in Los Feliz, blur the line between a hyper-casual restaurant and an ordering window. But Yuca's years-old traditions have caught the eyes of the James Beard Foundation, which gave it an American Classics award for its amazing food and longtime service to the neighborhood.

The All Flavor No Grease stand in Watts. *Noam Bleiweiss.*

Street food operations like these can spend years as solo ventures, with one person standing on the same corner every night, making the same dish or two for increasingly long lines of patient eaters. They may also expand, add a few outdoor folding tables or move into a better location, but in many cases, these are vendors that can be counted on for their location, their quality and their consistency. Here's where to find them.

TIRE SHOP TAQUERIA

Open: evenings and late night, primarily weekends
Location: South Avalon Boulevard, between East Fortieth Place and East Forty-
first Street, South L.A.

A more recent addition to Los Angeles's taco tradition, the so-called Tire Shop Taqueria wasted no time in adding itself to the necessary lexicon of anyone who is serious about street Mexican food. Pushed off the street and into the parking lot confines of (what else) a tire shop in Los Angeles's once worrisome but rapidly changing South Central neighborhood, this

Griddling handmade tortillas at the Tire Shop Taqueria. *Farley Elliott.*

standalone late-night option is doing Tijuana-influenced carne asada tacos at the highest levels.

Watching each station work in this long chain of taco creation offers a bit of magic in itself. First, there are the ladies up front, hand-pressing tortillas essentially to order and slapping them on the griddle to firm up just enough. Behind them, the man of action: he receives the fully cooked meat (usually carne asada) from the man past him who works the grill, gives it all an effortlessly quick chop into bite-size portions and then sets about the most important task of all. In one swoop, asada lands inside a warm tortilla, which is then dashed with sliced raw white onion and cilantro and then given a wide splash of thin guacamole. The whole thing is wrapped up like a cone in deli paper, with the open end showing layers of meat beneath a wash of puréed avocados.

Grab a seat at one of the few available tables and enjoy. Quesadillas, mulitas and other cuts of meat are available, but for the most authentic experience, order up a round of carne asada tacos. Then, when you've finished, hop in line for a few more.

LOS ANGELES STREET FOOD

ELOTE CORN MAN

Open: evenings and late nights
Location: Workman Street, between North Broadway and Manitou Avenue,
*   Lincoln Heights*

Corn has a long, if surprising, history as street food in Los Angeles. It's a popular afterschool snack for inner-city Latino kids looking to pour on some calories before dinner and can be seen on street corner after street corner while driving around town. The preparation for street corn, known as elote, is a simple one but no less delicious.

Whole ears of corn are grilled to a perfect tenderness, with a few blackened bites here and there to mix things up. Once finished, a smear of mayonnaise and wash of simple cojita cheese is common, as is a dusting of chile de arbol. Pressed through with a stick for easy carry and consumption, elote is a cheap, delicious street snack from Mexico that has made its way north.

And that's where the Lincoln Heights Elote Man comes in. The nearly three-decade-old elotero has amassed an almost cult-like following, with people waiting (and waiting) to grab a cob of his $1.50 corn. Doused in lime juice and not grilled, the Lincoln Heights Elote Man offers a slightly different experience than traditional operations peddling similar products, but the results are always the same: maximum deliciousness for a minimum price.

MAMA MUSUBI

Open: check @mamamusubiLA for times
Location: various farmers' markets and catering events

Though mostly a food festival and farmers' market staple, Mama Musubi is worth seeking out. The catering company's namesake dish, musubi (also widely known as onigiri), is a Japanese rice snack that has enjoyed a surge of recent popularity in America. Look through the emojis on your phone, and you'll notice a little musubi in the food section—it's the rounded white

Opposite: A gourmet plate of elote. *Farley Elliott.*

triangle with the little green strip (that's seaweed) holding everything together at the bottom.

At Mama Musubi, these rice balls are made as approachable as possible. Rather than just being the dense, starchy snack they seem, the musubi here is a handheld delight, each stuffed with an ingredient of choice. There's a wide array of upgraded options like miso Jidori chicken and Berkshire pork belly. The rice itself is folded in with a bit of Japanese nori and studded with sesame seeds before being wrapped in a final layer of seaweed. The results are undeniable, with each satisfying bite offering something akin to a heftier sushi roll, but better.

Tracking down the Mama Musubi team may take a bit of effort—their sometimes erratic schedule sees them volley between the far north farmers' market in Altadena and downtown stops, with a few Asian night markets and standalone pop-ups thrown in for good measure. But if you're looking to land a truly refined version of the popular Tokyo street food snack, there's likely no better place in Los Angeles.

BIGMISTA'S

Open: check @BigmistasBBQ for times
Location: various farmers' markets and catering events, plus Bigmista's Barbecue
   & Sammich Shop in Long Beach

It's not often that barbecue makes a list of best street foods. True, the often messy meal could be consumed on a picnic table outside or as little tide-you-over nibbles while standing in an excruciatingly long line to get inside the actual restaurant. But barbecue as pure street food? Not exactly.

Yet that's where Bigmista's fits right in, oddly enough. The larger-than-life Neil "Bigmista" Strawder has been cooking up his hodgepodge brand of L.A. barbecue for nearly half a decade, serving locals at farmers' markets around the county and wherever else he's asked to show up. The barbecue competition competitor doesn't need a restaurant all his own—just a smoker, some work space and a bunch of hungry customers.

Funnily enough, it's that do-it-yourself dynamic that has since allowed Strawder to actually open his own restaurant down in Long Beach while refusing to let go of his out-in-the-wild roots. Bigmista's brisket, pastrami, fried pork skin and desserts can still be found at farmers' markets from

A full plate at Bigmista's. *Farley Elliott*

Atwater Village to downtown Los Angeles. It's a grab-and-go operation, with no tables to speak of and the sun beating down. Less than optimal conditions for barbecue? Maybe in anyone else's hands. But for Neil Strawder's Bigmista, it's just another day on the clock.

PRANOM THAI

Open: evenings and late night
Location: various bars and pop-up locations

True Thai street food, cooked in a wok from a single burner out under the night sky, is no longer just a dream in Los Angeles—though it is cooked by one. Dream Kasestatad (yes, that's his real name) is the sole operator behind Pranom, a mostly pad Thai pop-up operation that's been working in front of bars, coffee shops and storefronts for several years.

Kasestatad, who grew up learning to cook from his family in Texas, does street Thai food his way. There's the single looming ring burner, gassed up by a propane tank, and the oversized wok used to sear ingredients and prep final dishes. Next to that is a simple set up: one table holds prepared

dry ingredients, sauces and whatever utensils are needed to enjoy that night's meal.

Options might range, on a given night, from souped-up chicken and shrimp pad Thai to the heftier pad see ew and, on occasion, khao soi. The latter is a Burmese-influenced noodle soup dish made with egg noodles, freshly cut greens and plenty of chili oil. It's the sort of warming post-drinking snack that is popular in Thailand but still has a ways to go in America.

Still, Kasestatad is among the only ones making such street dishes at all, which is novel in itself. The timing of his Pranom pop-ups varies wildly, and he often crisscrosses the city on a whim. He's best caught up with on Twitter to find out the next location of his late-night stops. Just get there early because Pranom tends to sell out.

Blue Corn Quesadilla Lady

Open: afternoons and early evening, primarily weekends
Location: Echo Park Avenue, between Sunset Boulevard and Park Avenue, Echo Park

Echo Park's so-called Blue Corn Quesadilla Lady is something of a legend. Having been peddling her regionally specific Oaxacan-style quesadillas from a small griddle cart for more than half a decade, the always unnamed entrepreneur has earned a cult-like following in Los Angeles. She can certainly be hard to track down, however.

With nothing to distinguish her visually from the occasional other small carts that populate near the corner of Sunset Boulevard and Echo Park Avenue in the heart of L.A.'s Echo Park neighborhood, the Blue Corn Quesadilla Lady relies instead on a healthy stream of locals who know her by sight and intrepid eaters willing to seek her out. As coverage of the one-woman cart has grown over the years, so have the lines, which makes it a bit easier to find the right cart on those days when she's actually out on the streets (there are no set times, locations or dates for the Blue Corn Quesadilla Lady—only hope).

Opposite, top: Pranom's Dream Kasestatad. *Noam Bleiweiss.*

Opposite, bottom: Pad Thai noodles in the wok at Pranom. *Dream Kasestatad.*

Echo Park's Blue Corn Quesadilla Lady. *Farley Elliott.*

Once found, however, its clear that nearby imitators pale in comparison. Working in small batches using blue corn masa—hence the unique blue tortilla look that has made the Lady so famous—these hand-patted Oaxacan quesadillas are about as authentic as you'll find. Oaxacan string cheese gets layered into a melty mess as the tortilla beneath it firms up, while ingredients like chorizo and potatoes or squash blossoms form the simple interior. One can even spring for the huitlacoche, a sort of funky corn-based option that's widely considered to be the truffles of southern Mexico. Slash the top with whatever salsa you choose and enjoy the show as the Blue Corn Quesadilla Lady tosses on another handmade tortilla for the customer behind you.

THE STREET FOOD LANDSCAPE IN LOS ANGELES TODAY

La Reyna Taco Table

Open: late night
Location: East Seventh Street at Mateo Street, Arts District, Downtown

As downtown Los Angeles continues to evolve, one taco stand remains a constant: La Reyna. The longtime street taco stand actually occupies the sidewalk in front of a dingy restaurant of the same name, which now acts essentially as overflow seating for the outdoor operation and nothing more. It's generally a sign of quality street food in Los Angeles when the stand out front is more popular than the restaurant it sits in front of.

Every night of the week, La Reyna serves its one-dollar, palm-sized tacos to waiting customers. Some are longtime regulars, crawling through downtown on their way home after a long day. Others are destination diners who make the occasional trip to La Reyna based on word of mouth. And still more are emerging all the time from the nearby mixed-use buildings and loft spaces of downtown's revitalized Arts District, which is perhaps the hottest destination for shopping, art and cuisine in town. The changing demographics thankfully haven't washed away the Queen (the English translation of La Reyna). Instead, she's as strong as ever.

The nightly al pastor game is strong here, thanks to a rotating fiery spit that delivers great bites of pork in each taco. Carne asada is another classic option, while lesser-known cuts like cabeza don't receive as much attention. There is no wrong choice here, though, as the salsa bar plays a great equalizer. Enticing slasa verdes and rojas offer mix-and-match possibilities with the otherwise unadorned tacos, and the offer of griddled onions and Serrano peppers is a welcome addition. At La Reyna, you can go as spicy or as delicate as you like. This longtime downtown street stand isn't here to judge.

Tacos Los Poblanos

Open: late night, primarily weekends
Location: South Central Avenue, between East Fifty-seventh Street and Slauson Avenue, South L.A.

Grilled meats are a barrier breaker. Nearly every culture has its own version of cooking animal proteins over open flame and, usually, charcoal, resulting in a uniqueness of place but familiarity of taste. It's possible to eat charcoal-grilled elk in Canada and smoky chicken in Peru and understand the common thread behind each.

It's that singularity of flavor that makes the late-night Los Poblanos taco operation just off Central Avenue in South L.A. such a hit. For anyone who eats meat, there's a commonality in every bite. Locals line up to watch the Pueblan-born taqueros deftly chop up endless piles of grilled carne asada, then slide the ingredients into a freshly cooked tortilla and slay the entire hand-sized taco with a well-mashed, thin guacamole. These are Tijuana-style tacos, but they also speak to this place, in this time, in this city. At Tacos Los Poblanos, it's easy to speak a common tongue.

LET'S BE FRANK

Open: *midday and evenings*
Location: *various pop-up locations, often at the Helms Bakery Complex in Culver City*

In all of the competition that comes with being a street food vendor, what's often lost is the conversation behind the ingredients themselves. Serving one-dollar tacos generally means using ingredients that are less than sustainable and likely have a murky sourcing background—to say nothing of the staff pay that comes from working on a truck selling those cheap tacos.

At Let's Be Frank, the conversation about sourcing, about ingredients, is front and center. It's the reason it has the name that it does. As a small hot dog cart willing to be frank about the meat it uses and the process for delivering the finished product to customers, Let's Be Frank stands alone.

Of course, it helps that the hot dogs are fantastic, too. Fresh dogs, either all grass-fed beef or a mix of beef and heritage pork, are worked up on a sizzling griddle from inside the bright red catering cart. Soy veggie dogs, turkey dogs and spicy sausages are also available, of course, with a wide array of possible toppings like fiery hot sauce and grilled onions. Each nitrate-, hormone- and antibiotic-free frank is cooked to order, so don't expect a grab-and-go experience, but the wait is more than worthwhile.

Opposite: The Let's Be Frank hot dog trailer. *Courtesy Let's Be Frank.*

LOS ANGELES STREET FOOD

MacArthur Park Tamale Vendors

Open: midday and evenings
Location: MacArthur Park, Westlake

MacArthur Park is, in many ways, an anomaly for Los Angeles. A bit of lush, verdant green in the middle of the city, the park is nearly 150 years old—an absolute rarity for just about anything in the city. It's designated as a Historic Cultural Monument and still—improbably, given the years of drought—sports a large water feature. It is, in many ways, an urban oasis.

Unfortunately, the park has in more recent decades also been an oasis for the seedier side of Los Angeles. For years, drugs and violence marred the park, making even the daytime questionable for tourists and anyone unfamiliar with the area. That's been changing though, if slowly, as rampant homelessness and gang violence gives way to mom-and-pop street vendors and an array of daytime activities. Slowly, the park is offering more to the community and getting back plenty in return.

Today's MacArthur Park is still gritty and can be a bit dirty at the edges, but for anyone willing to dive into the culture there, amazing regional cuisine awaits. The primary example is tamales. A largely Central American and Mexican tradition, rice and milled corn form the most common base for tamales, which are steamed slowly either in banana leaves or corn husks. Each contains a thin river of ingredients inside its steamed pouch, from shredded beef to vegetables to sweeter options like pineapple. Most of the vendors here are some level of Central American (they're often Guatemalan), which can make for a fun couple hours of cart-hopping through the park.

As with any area still in the throes of a more positive change following decades of drug use and crime, exercise caution when visiting MacArthur Park. Or, more appropriately, just use some common sense to ensure a great afternoon of eating.

All Flavor No Grease

Open: midday and evenings
Location: East 108th Street, between Stanford and McKinley Avenues, Watts

Keith Garrett didn't always have plans to open his own street food brand out of his parents' driveway in Watts. The looming local spent years doing various jobs but never truly found a passion that called to him. Eventually, after a lifetime of eating local Mexican food (and largely being disappointed with the results), Garrett decided to see if he could cook up some proper burritos, tacos and quesadillas himself.

The result is All Flavor No Grease, a daily pop-up of sorts based off 108th Street in a little-seen part of South Los Angeles. Garrett's food plays like something adjacent to fast food but with a higher level of ingredients (he breaks down beef shoulder himself for the carne asada) and dedication. Quesadillas are massively thick, stuffed with everything from spiced potatoes to chicken, cheese and pico de gallo, while burritos become rolled-up versions of the same. This is hot sauce—laden, cheesy, sour cream–infused Mexican food—forget what your Mexican grandmother taught you.

So far, it's been a winning combination for Garrett, whose All Flavor No Grease Instagram account

Keith Garrett of All Flavor No Grease in Watts. *Noam Bleiweiss*.

has racked up more than ten thousand followers. People drive from hours away to enjoy the curbside cooking being done here, and it's not hard to see why. While far from being anything "authentic," Garrett's food is absolutely delicious.

YUCA'S

Open: 11:00 a.m. to 6:00 p.m., Monday through Saturday
Location: Hillhurst Avenue, between Ambrose Avenue and Price Street, Los Feliz

Though bordering on full restaurant territory, Yuca's in Los Feliz remains primarily a takeaway stand with a few crowded tables orbiting nearby. Need

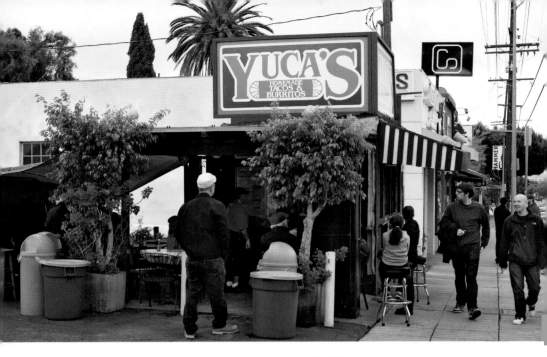

The James Beard Award–winning Yuca's in Los Feliz. *Paul Bartunek.*

shade? If it's available, you'll find it under the iconic blue tarp attached to one side of the shack, which sits in the parking lot of a liquor store. Outside of those few seats, you're largely on your own.

That certainly hasn't stopped people from making the trek to this diminutive hut just off the main drag, which has been crafting its pull-apart pork cochinita pibil dishes since 1976. That's still the dish to order today, though the carne asada also works as a serviceable option, if only largely because of its heft. The tacos here are thick, pliant and large, thoroughly dwarfing their one-dollar taco truck cousins and with a price to match.

If you've got it in you, consider ordering the burger here as well. It's a sleeper hit with locals, who know that the beef patties get worked over on the same griddle as all that Mexican food, which means nothing but amazing flavor for the finished product. After all, there's a reason this little Los Feliz bungalow kitchen earned a James Beard Award as a true American Classic.

Chapter 11
Trucks and Trailers

I n Los Angeles, there is a proliferation of truly mobile operators, filling
out the fat middle of L.A.'s street food belly. Many, though certainly not
all, operate as aboveboard businesses, complete with health ratings and tax
payments. They may have a Twitter account or Facebook page, but for most

Ordering at the El Chato taco truck. *Paul Bartunek.*

trucks, it's the workaday life that keeps them in business. Using familiar parking spots, keeping a routine—it's the kind of day-in and day-out work that keeps many trucks flying under the radar, happily catering to a local clientele that they've built over the years.

This motley street army is the most recognizable face of today's street food movement. The lonchero itself, a catering truck often immortalized as a bit rough around the edges, dinged up and covered in stickers or a colorful mural, is perhaps the best visual symbol of street food there is. It's a model that's been copied in dozens of cities across America in the past decade but has existed in L.A. for generations.

These trucks and trailers are ubiquitous, operating thousands at a time every single day in every part of the county. Notwithstanding strict residential neighborhoods or areas with tight parking regulations, it's almost impossible to avoid routinely spotting these trucks as they crawl to and from their commissary kitchens or as they set up shop in front of car washes, construction sites and closed-up auto body shops.

Of course, the numbers only climb after dark. The popular late-night options not only sit in as an effective solution to an evening of drinking, but they are also for many a final meal for the day, served with love and at a price point that is unattainable outside of the fast-food industry. Any Angeleno with a year or two under his or her belt has a favorite taco truck or two; if

A taco cart in Highland Park. *Paul Bartunek.*

Street tacos off Pico Boulevard. *Paul Bartunek.*

he's smart, he has one for every neighborhood. After all, these are the sort of cheesy, greasy, late-night spots that have gotten, collectively, an entire city through a few rough nights.

For this and other acts of culinary benevolence, it is possible for these trucks and trailers to, on occasion, become recognized with a certain amount of respect around town. First, a neighborhood finds its own perfect vendor (or rather the vendor finds a perfectly hungry neighborhood), and the residents prop it up with nightly visits, earning hordes of devotees in the process. Maybe somewhere along the way a chatty food writer shows up to try to earn the next great street food scoop, camera in tow and ready to tell the world. Maybe a celebrity food and travel television show host swings through, and before you know it the 1:00 a.m. lines go from lengthy to absolutely unbearable.

It's impossible to say how these things get started, but eventually, some of the best trucks do earn a sense of fame, at least in Los Angeles. Most of the operators you'll pass as you cross the city by car, however, are destined not for fame but for consistency. These trailers and trucks are the real workhorses of Los Angeles's street food game. At once fiercely proud and worthy of the loyalty they receive, it is this level of on-the-street dining that makes L.A. so unique from the rest of the nation. Their plates of tacos are our city's version of a calling card, one that we as a community are happy to dial up a few times a week.

These are the best trucks and trailers you can eat at right now.

Prepping tacos from Ricky's Fish Taco. *Paul Bartunek.*

RICKY'S FISH TACO

Open: midday, primarily weekends
Location: North Virgil Avenue, between Sunset Boulevard and De Longpre
  Avenue, Silver Lake

There is perhaps no more approachable taco truck in Los Angeles than Ricky's Fish Taco. The matte gray catering truck parks just off the street on Virgil Avenue in Silver Lake, with rotating but trustworthy midday hours. Any variations in the schedule (this is still a taco truck, after all) are handled via Twitter by Ricky Piña himself, the namesake Ensenada, Mexico native who rose to prominence with a series of semi-legal fish-frying operations around town. The @RickysFishTacos Twitter handle now has thousands of followers and shows no signs of slowing down.

Ricky's is a lunchtime lonchero, so don't expect heavy late-night options dripping with cheese, red meat and beans. As in Ensenada itself, lightly fried white fish and shrimp compose the menu (though options like lobster are occasionally available), battered and dipped with care before being served on a warmed tortilla and topped with a shredded cabbage slaw. Doctor each taco with squirts from the crema and salsa bottles and then grab an aguas frescas to wash it all down.

THE STREET FOOD LANDSCAPE IN LOS ANGELES TODAY

El Chato

Open: late night, except Sunday
Location: La Brea at Olympic Boulevard, Mid-City

For years, the El Chato taco truck was hidden in plain sight. Occupying some prime (if a bit unconventional, for a street food operation) real estate at the busy corner of La Brea Avenue and Olympic Boulevard just south of the famed Miracle Mile, El Chato initially drew only local crowds. The dim white trailer dutifully served up its version of the L.A. Mexican street food trinity: tacos, burritos and quesadillas. In 2009, things began to change.

El Chato's rise coincides with the popularity of gourmet food trucks, which gave regular folks the confidence to eat from street trucks and trailers and the willingness to drive for the experience. Soon, food writers like Jonathan

The El Chato taco truck. *Paul Bartunek.*

Gold were stopping by and waiting in the ever-increasing line, queuing up for the spit-roasted and griddle-finished al pastor, stuffed into tortillas large and small. Here the burritos and quesadillas may be nearly as popular as the one-dollar tacos, a rare sight in Los Angeles. There's something about the larger, meatier options that appeal to the late-night crowd, which lines up regularly for twenty-minute waits.

Food is served until the wee hours of the morning, with the surrounding parking lot (by day, the land belongs to an auto body shop) filling up fast with cars that quickly double as makeshift tables for the weighty plates of food. In-the-know diners make sure to ask for extra helpings of the smoky salsa, with slow-cooked onions on the side. And beware the bowl of raw onions and strips of habanero sitting out by the napkins: it packs a wallop.

Tacos Leo

Open: late night
Location: La Brea at Venice Boulevard, Mid-City

Tacos Leo is a longtime darling of the late-night dining scene in Los Angeles and on weekends commands the sort of requisite lines for such a position. The truck, with attached weekend stand, specializes in al pastor tacos—that slowly marinating pork option that has come to largely define the city's Mexican street food. At other vendors, lesser cuts of meat are given little respect, leading to inconsistent tacos that, even on their best day, rely on cheap products and unskilled taqueros.

At Tacos Leo, everything is top notch. The worker manning the spinning al pastor trompo could work a circus act with the deft way he handles the blade, peeling off thin sheets of perfectly timed pork and layering them piece by piece onto a waiting tortilla. Another flick of the wrist and off comes a wedge of pineapple from the top of the spit, flying through the air before landing perfectly in the center of the waiting taco. It's a sight to behold, and hundreds of customers do just that nightly.

While the vertical al pastor spit isn't out nightly (wait for the weekend to enjoy that), the meat here suffers no less for it. Tacos (burritos, quesadillas and more are offered as well, but Los Angeles is unequivocally a taco town) are ordered and paid for up front and then received a few minutes

Customers at the Tacos Leo truck. *Liezl Estipona.*

later as unadorned discs, ready to be dressed from the nearby salsa bar. Options abound depending on one's taste and heat preferences, though the lack of seating brings everyone together at once, huddled over their paper plates, tightly gripping the next taco bite lest it all fall apart.

Tacos Tamix

Open: late night
Location: West Pico Boulevard, between South Longwood Avenue and San Vicente Boulevard, Mid-City

Oftentimes, being second best is worth a trophy all its own. Tacos Tamix, a transient Pico Boulevard taco truck, is known for its al pastor. The only problem is, so is nearby competitor Tacos Leo. Alone, each operation would have its merits, but it's impossible not to compare the two given

Ordering at the Tacos Tamix truck. *Liezl Estipona.*

their overlapping menu and proximity—most nights, Tamix parks on Pico Boulevard just two blocks from the ever-popular Tacos Leo.

At Tamix, the pastor is sliced a little thicker, the marinade a little stronger than at Tacos Leo. It's one reason the weekend pastor spit tends to sell out; taqueros here give the people what they want, and lots of it. There may be less skill in the practice and balance in the execution of an al pastor taco from Tamix as opposed to Tacos Leo, but in reality, the differences aren't so egregious as to be unforgivable. Many late-night diners, overcome by the prospect of spending dozens of minutes in line for tacos from Leo, head to Tamix for a quicker fix, debating the merits of one over the other while clearly making their choice over a plate of Tamix pastor.

THE STREET FOOD LANDSCAPE IN LOS ANGELES TODAY

TACOS LOS GÜICHOS

Open: late night and midday on weekends
Location: West Slauson Avenue at Broadway, South L.A.

As South Los Angeles's demographics continue to change, so too does its cuisine. Mexican food now shares equal space with the usual array of burger joints, Creole restaurants, barbecue stops and soul food options. And on the streets, the numbers are overwhelming: Mexican food is everywhere after dark, and it's only gaining prominence.

Then again, not every popular street taco stop needs to pop up after dark. Tacos Los Güichos was for years a daytime operation only, serving pounds of pork carnitas to anyone who swung through. The simple parking lot operation utilizes a painted trailer for walk-up orders, while the dedicated carnitas man works his trade a few feet away using dedicated equipment. Anything non-pork is cooked directly on the truck, but you won't find many folks opting for the carne asada or chicken; they're too busy ringing the bubbling cazo filled with all manner of pork products, picking their favorite cuts and chatting it up with the man who works the pot, slowly turning the meat as it crisps and cooks.

Carnitas here is a long game, with pig parts cooked through over hours inside of boiling fat (usually lard) and served piecemeal as tacos composed of different parts. Anything from shoulder to skin to snout is available, and if you just can't decide, there's always the mixto, a chef's choice blend of cooked meats.

Prepping the carnitas at Tacos Los Güichos. *Paul Bartunek.*

Carnitas from the cazo at Tacos Los Güichos. *Paul Bartunek.*

Better still, Tacos Los Güichos recently started running a late-night al pastor spit to complement its daytime carnitas. It's rare that one crew can work two completely different specialties with success, but Los Güichos seems to have found a way, making it a twice-a-day option for anyone in the neighborhood or willing to make the drive.

MARISCOS JALISCO

Open: midday
Location: East Olympic Boulevard, between South Evergreen Avenue and South Dacotah Street, Boyle Heights

Raul Ortega is a man of conviction. As the longtime purveyor of one of the city's finest taco trucks, Mariscos Jalisco in East L.A., Ortega works tirelessly to make sure his ceviches, tacos dorados and tostadas are as well received one day as they are the next. The popular street food figure began his culinary

Above: The Mariscos Jalisco truck. *Paul Bartunek.*

Below: Seafood tostada in East L.A. *Paul Bartunek.*

life selling tacos on the streets of San Juan de los Lagos in his home state of Jalisco, Mexico, eventually immigrating to the United States to begin a life in Los Angeles.

The passion for service never left him, though, and carries through in everything that Ortega does to make his truck a success. The most popular menu item by far, the fried shrimp tacos dorados, are perhaps Los Angeles's single best taco, a perfectly realized mix of fresh marinated seafood wrapped in a crispy tortilla shell and topped with slightly spicy salsa and a few slices of cooling avocado. It's the sort of simple, well-executed dish that is so ubiquitous to Mexican street food.

There are other seafood dishes available on the tight menu at Mariscos Jalisco, from simple ceviches to tall piles of seafood plated onto crispy tortilla tostadas. The most famous of these is the Poseidon, a "king of the sea" type of order that combines just about every aquatic animal on one tostada. It's meant for sharing, of course, but with food this delicious, there are no guarantees.

CARNITAS EL MOMO

Open: midday, primarily on weekends
Location: South Avalon Boulevard, between East Sixtieth Street and East Sixty-
  first Street, South L.A.

Carnitas El Momo captured hearts and tastebuds back in 2013 thanks largely to Bill Esparza, the longtime street eater well known for his Mexican food leanings. Esparza hipped the city to the unstoppable slow-cooked pork parts coming from this simple trailer, which serves up its carnitas in the style of Guanajuato, Mexico.

At El Momo, it's all about the pig, in its many sticky, crispy forms. Copper cazos are still used to slowly boil everything from the hoof to the heart, using pork fat as a cooking base to meld the flavors together. Like other carnitas operators, "Momo" Acosta—the namesake man from Guanajuanto who gave rise to this carnitas legend in Los Angeles—doesn't skimp on details; pork renders until it's done, and not a moment sooner, which can occasionally make opening and closing times a bit…imprecise.

Still, the occasional wait is more than worth it. Piles of savory pork are doled out piecemeal depending on your cut of choice (for beginners, the

The Carnitas El Momo truck. *Farley Elliott.*

shoulder and belly are good places to start, while the snout and ears offer some interesting contrast). Slap the ingredients into a tortilla and finish as you please. Just do it quickly, as there's probably a line behind you.

SUPER TORTAS D.F.

Open: evenings and late night, primarily weekends
Location: South Central Avenue at East Forty-first Street, South L.A.

Named after Mexico City (*Distrito Federal*, as its commonly referred to in Mexico), Super Tortas D.F. is a fly-by-night Mexican sandwich operation known for sky-high creations and long late-evening lines. Its popularity is thanks largely to one man, Justino Gress, who mans the griddle inside the trailer nightly. A former Mexico City resident himself, where the torta is among the most revered street foods, Gress knows a thing or two about working heat, ingredients and time to create an effortlessly delicious sandwich that's actually anything but effortless.

Popular options like the Rusa combine a thinly pounded and fried beef cutlet with shreds of pork and lots of cheese, while more exotic takes include

Above: Tortas from the Super Tortas D.F. truck in South L.A. *Julia A. Reed.*

Below: The Super Tortas D.F. truck in South L.A. *Julia A. Reed.*

everything from pineapple to eggs. All are moderately priced at around six dollars each—even the Cubana, which is inarguably the most ordered menu item available at Super Tortas D.F. An outlandish take on the much more subdued Cuban sandwich known as a cubano, the massive Cubana here is layered with ham, egg, slices of hot dog, cheese, chorizo and that same fried beef cutlet, with enough greens and mayonnaise to match. It's a formidable thing, meant more to knock someone out than to fortify him for a night ahead.

Which makes the hours at Super Tortas D.F. so surprising. Super Tortas D.F. is far from a purely late-night operation, where foggy minds might over-order before quickly turning to bed. Gress is an artist, and he treats his product as such, only coming out to his well-known South L.A. corner in the late afternoon to catch commuters on their way home from work. Most nights, the cash-only spot is all packed up by 11:00 p.m.

Dollar Hits

Open: evenings and late night, primarily weekends
Location: West Temple Street, between North Carondelet Street and North Park View Street, Historic Filipinotown

Street food abounds in Manila, the muggy capital of the Philippines. But thousands of miles away in Los Angeles, Filipino cuisine operates mostly indoors, tucked into tiny storefront restaurants in enclave neighborhoods like Eagle Rock, where first- and second-generation Filipinos can gather to dine and engage in a common culture.

As the largest Asian minority group in all of California, Filipino cuisine certainly isn't hard to come by—except on the street. That's part of what makes Dollar Hits, a dedicated late-night stop in Historic Filipinotown, so exciting. Operating as both a truck and adjacent charcoal grilling station, this meat skewer specialist provides a rare taste of Manila on the streets of L.A. Rather than cooking your food in front of you from the trusty confines of the truck, Dollar Hits does little more than hand over one-dollar meat skewers and let you do the work yourself. Place your order and take your meats to one of the nearby grills to cook them up as needed—this is street food at its simplest.

Fish balls, pig ears and more common cuts can all be found pre-skewered and ready to be ordered off of a printed call sheet, while sauces and drinks

The ordering table at Dollar Hits. *Matthew Kang.*

weigh down the table in front of the truck. Balut, the often off-putting Pinoy egg dish, can also be found here. But like the congealed pork blood cubes, it's only for the strong of stomach.

TAMALES ELENA

Open: midday
Location: Wilmington Avenue at 110th Street, Watts

Once a sort of shorthand for crime and inequality in Los Angeles, the South L.A. neighborhood of Watts has become something of a culinary street food destination. Thanks in part to changing demographics that have shown a stark increase in Mexican and Central American immigrants moving to the relatively inexpensive area, Watts now enjoys an emerging street food tradition that is worth seeking out.

Of note in the area is Tamales Elena, which is on Wilmington Avenue near 110th Street. The unassuming trailer does, as its name implies, tamales exclusively, made in the style of Guerrero, Mexico. While the hyper-regional specifics between tamale styles are a conversation for another time, know this: the version found at Tamales Elena is among the best in Los Angeles.

THE STREET FOOD LANDSCAPE IN LOS ANGELES TODAY

Made basically to order rather than prepped and steamed well in advance, each long, nearly cylindrical tamal bursts with warm, soft, airy masa. Inside, various cuts of meat are offered, with chicken and pork the main players (beef, when found in tamales, tends to be shredded in order to keep from being too chewy or dry). Cheese and corn are also popular options, and it's even possible to enjoy dessert from the same truck, as pineapple and strawberry fillings give the option for a bit of sweetness instead.

Los Originales Tacos Arabes de Puebla

Open: evenings and late night, primarily weekends
Location: East Olympic Boulevard, between Esperanza Street and Mirasol
  Street, Boyle Heights

Just when you thought you knew all there was to know about tacos in Mexico (and, by some extension, Los Angeles), along comes the tacos Arabes. A hyper-specific regional variation that enjoys the most popularity in Puebla, southeast of Mexico City, tacos Arabes take just about everything familiar to tacos and give them a bit of a tweak.

Rather than grilling meats and placing them inside of a smallish corn tortilla, tacos Arabes tend to rely on a vertical spit that slowly roasts the meat of choice. Lamb is popular, as is marinated pork, with charcoal acting as a major player in the cooking process, imbuing its traditional smokiness. Instead of corn tortillas, tacos Arabes apply a base that is akin to Middle Eastern flatbread; it's thicker, larger and more pliant overall, relying on flour instead of corn masa for a bit of bubble and rise, somewhat like a pita.

Early versions of the taco Arabes style are rumored to have come in the early 1900s from Lebanese and Iraqi immigrants (the same group that, apparently, has given the world al pastor), who tweaked their traditional gyro recipes to suit their new clientele. Now, the large, rolled tacos enjoy chipotle and other regional salsas rather than any yogurt-based topping but are still prepared in largely the same manner as a gyro might be.

Which brings us to Los Angeles. Parked on Olympic Boulevard, Los Originales Tacos Arabes de Puebla is a popular late-evening truck that utilizes the full history of its Pueblan ancestry to bring the popular street snack to the States. Simple shaved slices of spit-roasted pork layer the inside of a wide, filling flatbread tortilla, with little more to accompany the flavors than a thick spread of mild salsa roja. Stringy Oaxacan cheese and slices of avocado are another popular addition, though no one will blame you for just downing the mini burrito–sized tacos in unadorned platefuls.

El Matador

Open: evenings and late night
Location: North Western Avenue at Lexington Avenue, East Hollywood

El Matador is often considered to be Hollywood's premier taco truck, though it doesn't park within a mile of the well-known Walk of Fame. The Hollywood tourist core is too pricey, too well trafficked for a worn old lonchero to set up shop from 6:00 p.m. until 4:00 a.m. Besides, there are plenty of on-site restaurants that would make a fuss (to say nothing of the roving bacon-wrapped hot dog carts that congregate outside clubs on the weekends).

Instead, El Matador occupies a bit of asphalt down Western Avenue, near the intersection with Santa Monica Boulevard. The daytime auto body shop makes for a perfect late-night taco stop. It's so perfect, in fact, that a second

Tacos from the El Matador truck in East Hollywood. *Jakob N. Layman.*

truck also parks in the same lot, no more than twenty feet away. Both seem to get along well enough, but it's El Matador that sports the longer lines and the beloved local devotion, especially among weekend drinkers at the cocktail bar across the street.

If looking straight at the auto body shop, El Matador is the truck on the left—or just look for the faded lettering on the hood. Once certain you've landed the right lonchero, step up to the order window and fire away, using the menu board on the side of the truck as a guiding tool. Almost everything here is worthwhile, especially if you've had a few yourself, but the best of the bunch are the asada, stewed chicken and buche, a softer cut of tripe that comes from the insides of the cow. It's not for the faint of heart, but the mineraly flavor pairs well with a strong salsa, which El Matador definitely has.

La Estrella

Open: midday, evening and late night
Location: York Boulevard, between North Avenue 53 and North Avenue 54,
  Highland Park

There may be no more trusted name in late-night taco eating than La Estrella, the Eastside institution with a few sit-down restaurants (and at least one truck) to its name. The most famous of the La Estrellas is undoubtedly the mobile one. Or *non*-mobile, as the case may be: La Estrella's truck on York in Highland Park sits off the street in a permanent spot. It even has its own sign pole, despite being just a truck.

This is the La Estrella that draws lines down the block on late weekend nights. It's the La Estrella that locals take newcomers to when they want to show off their neighborhood taco joint. And it's the same La Estrella that comes up in any conversation about tacos in Highland Park, which is quite a feat for an L.A. neighborhood that is absolutely overrun with Mexican food.

To order at La Estrella, just step up onto the wooden platform (it's an elevation thing, since the truck sits so high off the street) to order up from the usual assortment: cabeza, buche, carnitas, carne asada. Tortas and burritos are possible but not advised; here, it's best to stick with the tacos. Served full with the meat of choice and just waiting to be covered in a sneakily hot salsa of your choice, these diminutive street tacos are the sort of backbone meal that tens of thousands of Angelenos rely on every day.

EL TAQUITO MEXICANO

Open: evenings and late night
Location: Fair Oaks Avenue, between Palmetto Drive and West California
  Boulevard, Pasadena

Pasadena's premier taco truck, El Taquito Mexicano, is also one of its oldest. The late-night operator has been firing up its grills since 1979, which in Los Angeles food terms is several lifetimes away. After nearly fifteen years in business, El Taquito relocated to its current position along Fair Oaks Avenue, a major thoroughfare in the quickly expanding L.A. suburb, which provided a lot more visibility and increased foot traffic.

The twenty-year-old move seems to have paid off. El Taquito is among the busiest late-night places to eat in all of Pasadena—truck or not. A

A full plate of carnitas tacos. *Paul Bartunek.*

meal here is cheap and plentiful, buoyed by fantastic salsas and a team that knows how to expertly man the stoves. Even with prices hovering near $1.50 per street taco (most places in Los Angeles still land around $1.00), a meal can be had at El Taquito for ashtray change.

There are seven primary meat options aboard the no-frills truck, with asada the runaway favorite. However, in-the-know eaters tend to lean on the chicarrones, which (unlike the more common crispy, airy version found in pre-packaged gas station snack aisles) is a slow-cooked pig skin that offers a bit of chew and plenty of porky funk. Tacos like these are a mainstay in Mexico and not uncommon in many parts of Los Angeles, but discovering a perfect chicharron taco in Pasadena is a bit like winning the late-night lottery.

Tacos Quetzalcoatl

Open: midday
Location: East Olympic Boulevard at South Ferris Avenue, East Los Angeles

Vegetarianism isn't big in Mexico. Most often, it's an option born more out of convenience than choice. Pork is by far the most popular protein on plates throughout Mexico, with other vegetarian possibilities like huitlacoche (Mexican corn smut), potatoes and griddled peppers and onions jogging along far behind.

That hasn't stopped East L.A.'s Tacos Quetzacoatl from making a killing with its own non-meat taco options. It should be noted that there is, of course, meat on the menu, in the form of barbacoa, cecina and pancita, among others. But it's the veggie tacos that deserve the most respect here.

Greens proliferate at this weekend trailer (which sometimes floats in and out of parking spaces downtown, when the time is right). Mexico-specific ingredients like huauzontles (a sort of spiny green vegetable with allusions to broccoli) can be found here, along with more forthcoming veggies like spinach and squash. Anyone looking to get a day's fill of greens should land on the Omega 2, a cheekily named taco that emerges filled with mushrooms, squash, spinach, cheese and more.

LOS ANGELES STREET FOOD

TACOS CUERNAVACA

Open: evenings and late night
Location: Whittier Boulevard, between Belden Avenue and South Eastmont
Avenue, East L.A.

The nearly decade-old Tacos Cuernavaca has become something of an East L.A. legend, even along Whittier Boulevard, where trucks, stands and carts dot the nighttime landscape. As a solo operator in a crowded field of Mexican street food options, Tacos Cuernavaca was long ago forced to innovate. There's the colorful paint job, the bright lights strung along the top of the cab and an LED screen that scrolls slowly above the windshield, relaying the options (and the quality) offered on board.

What really puts Tacos Cuernavaca in a different league, though, is its menu. Hailing from the city of Cuernavaca in Mexico, a short trip southwest of Mexico City, Tacos Cuernavaca serves the sort of big-city street food one might normally expect, but with regional ambition. Regular tacos are possible here, as are huaraches, but the real dish on offer is the alambre—a do-it-yourself mixed plate of grilled onions, vegetables and assorted meats, fused together with melted cheese. Tortillas are provided on the side; crafting tacos from alambre mix is left entirely up to you.

For anyone feeling adventurous, Tacos Cuernavaca also occasionally produces a taco acorazado, otherwise known as the battleship taco. It's a fortified double tortilla stacked with Mexican rice and whatever meat is on hand, plus sour cream, cheese and peppers. It's not always available, but it's definitely worth asking.

LA ISLA BONITA

Open: midday, except Thursday
Location: Rose Avenue, between Third and Fourth Streets, Venice

Unlike beachy ocean towns along the nearby Baja Peninsula in northern Mexico, Los Angeles's waterfront is not exactly teeming with cheap street eats. There are a few trucks that brave the crowds of Santa Monica to park along the cliffs on Ocean Avenue or a bit farther south near the pier, but much of the sunset dining in the area is indoors, sit-down and rather pricey.

Tacos from the La Isla Bonita truck in Venice. *Noam Bleiweiss.*

In short: the real estate costs and parking prices keep most of the small fish from swimming too close to shore.

Just blocks from the beach in Venice, however, there is one intrepid lunchtime truck that dares to dream. It's La Isla Bonita, or the "beautiful island," and it acts as a lonely street taco benchmark for the area, just about the only one within shouting distance of the water. As such, locals line up early and often for a taste of the simple flavors at lunch time. There is seafood, of course, done up mostly by way of ceviches and mariscos tostadas with thick slices of avocado atop.

Mostly, though, La Isla Bonita is all about the land animals, be it beef or chicken. The asada is a bit smoky and chopped finely into small bits, then laced over top with creamy whole beans and a salsa roja that can get a bit fiery. Similarly, the chicken earns raves from longtime diners who form lines down the block. Chopped up into thick bites, the marinated bird is the perfect soft complement to fresh onions and cilantro. Tack on some of the slow-cooked onions, and you've got a simple plate of Mexican flavor to take straight to the beach. That's a surprising rarity in Los Angeles.

LOS ANGELES STREET FOOD

KEMBO TRUCK

Open: evenings and late night, except Sunday
Location: North Atlantic Boulevard, between West Emerson and Garvey
  Avenues, Monterey Park

Los Angeles's San Gabriel Valley is a culinary sight to behold. Canvasing a wide collection of suburban towns that spread east from downtown, the enormous landscape holds millions of ethnic Chinese, Taiwanese, Korean and Japanese families. And with those families, of course, come family restaurants, casual eateries and late-night dining experiences that aren't found anywhere else in the city.

The only real problem: they're all indoors. Thanks in part to the cheaper rents found in the SGV, as its known, there is little by way of food actually prepared on the street. Instead, small storefronts and unassuming second-floor restaurants abound, making for its own interweaving labyrinth of spots to be discovered. Then there is the Kembo truck, a late-night cart found in Monterey Park that is fully mobile—and therefore doesn't have much competition.

Parked in front of a Ralph's grocery store just off Atlantic Avenue, the Kembo truck is the work of chef Edward Hsu, a quiet Taiwanese man

The Kembo truck is the only Taiwanese street cart in Los Angeles. *Farley Elliott.*

Grilling meat and corn at the Kembo truck. *Farley Elliott.*

who wanted more than just the occasional taco truck roaming the streets he loved.

The resulting menu is heavy on the Taiwanese meat skewers, offered in chicken, beef or pork. They're five dollars for a bunch of five and are finished off with a salty-sweet blend of honey, soy sauce and a bit of spice. Snackier items include scored and grilled sausages, as well as fried sweet turnip cakes, fried fish cakes, simple tater tots and Taiwanese grilled sweet corn.

Made fresh on site and cooked to order, each dish at Kembo offers a peek into the street culture of places like China and Taiwan, where such delicacies are much more common. Chef Hsu is doing something wonderfully interesting with his Kembo truck and, in so doing, hopes to change perceptions that the San Gabriel Valley is a Los Angeles town where only Latino street food can thrive.

LOS ANGELES STREET FOOD

TACOS LA FONDA

Open: evenings and late night
Location: Vanowen Street at Vineland Avenue, North Hollywood

The San Fernando Valley is a sprawling mass of mostly low-slung buildings stretching north from the cultural center of Los Angeles. Often described as being over "the hill" (or hills, really, which indicates the relatively small Santa Monica and Verdugo Mountains), the Valley is a place for quiet family streets, suburban shopping malls and industrial zones made up of endless warehouses. It is also, due to cheap rent and cultural proliferation, home to many great meals.

Much like the San Gabriel Valley to the southeast, most of the best meals found in the San Fernando Valley are kept indoors, however. With space aplenty and a low cost per square foot for real estate, the advantages of permanent storage, guaranteed parking and a fully built-out kitchen are attractive enough to usually draw in even the smallest of small-time operators. There are still plenty of neighborhood-specific taco trucks, however, and chief among them is Tacos La Fonda.

Found almost every night on the northwest corner of Vanowen and Vineland, Tacos La Fonda is a colorful street vendor trailer outfitted with floodlights and one of the city's best salsa tables. Tortillas are hand made right on the truck and emerge from their time on the griddle as thick, warm discs, halfway between a tortilla and pita. They're massive, too, holding at least twice as much volume as what you'd find on most other trucks. That's good news for customers, who line up for thick, juicy strips of carne asada and griddle-cooked al pastor, plus the lesser-known cuts like buche (stomach), tripas (tripe, or organ meat) and cabeza (beef cheeks, mostly).

The best part of Tacos La Fonda, though? The salsa bar, which is practically overrun with large tubs of DIY ingredients, from freshly chopped onions and cilantro to warm, griddled onions and pico de gallo. Guacamole is available here, as is sour cream—a very unusual move in town. Unlike the Northern California Mexican food scene, which largely approximates what can be found at a nearby Chipotle, such dishes in Los

Opposite, top: The La Fonda taco truck. *Clay Larsen.*

Opposite, bottom: Tacos from the La Fonda taco truck. *Clay Larsen.*

Angeles are often much less cluttered with add-ons. No sour cream, no cheese, things like that. But the option at La Fonda is too good for many customers to pass up, which is why the truck goes through buckets of the stuff nightly.

Chapter 12
Gourmet Food Trucks

While usually working within the same technical limitations as the aforementioned trailers and loncheros, gourmet food trucks are a beast unto themselves. They operate differently, tend to draw in a different clientele and enjoy a largely different set of rewards, though there are drawbacks.

First rising to prominence between 2007 and 2008, gourmet trucks quickly grew to become their own viable market segment within the overall

The Komodo truck. *Jon Nguyen.*

restaurant landscape. Suddenly, talented cooks and chefs who lacked the bottom line to dive into the full restaurant game found themselves aboard colorfully wrapped catering trucks, outfitted to serve whatever cuisine formed the backbone of their concept. It's a notion made romantic by Roy Choi, the once hotel cook turned street food legend who used his wiles and his passion to reinvent the national street food scene with Kogi BBQ.

Like Kogi, many of these gourmet food trucks can be easily parsed out from their simpler taco truck counterparts based on menu alone. More often than not, the style is fusion cuisine, the pairing of often disparate cultural culinary influences in order to create a mashed-up new marriage that enhances the best notions from both. It's a simple idea that can be exceedingly hard to excel at, however, especially with little time to R&D recipes and low operating capital with which to stay afloat while the rest of the world catches on to their genius.

Of course, there are also more options within the gourmet food truck world than often seems possible with simpler trucks and carts. By eschewing "traditional" or "authentic" labels, enterprising chefs can work up entire new avenues with which to feed an increasingly inquisitive population. In the years that followed the initial food truck boom, everything from completely

A burger from the Lobos Truck. *Courtesy the Lobos Truck.*

organic red sauce Italian recipes to raw food to South African bunny chow found its way aboard all manner of truck and trailer.

Another notable difference: among non-gourmet trucks, English-language social media platforms like Twitter are still largely an anomaly. Conversely, Twitter was for years the medium of choice for food trucks looking to stay relevant with their clientele (though that's largely been supplanted by apps like Instagram now). And now, rather than posting an updated location just minutes before arriving and expecting the hungry masses to follow, most gourmet trucks rely on set schedules (and lots of private events) to keep their brand top of mind. By making the interaction with the customer as seamless as possible, gourmet trucks can hope for some repeat business the next time they swing through to a particular location on their predefined schedule.

To that end, one of the most enduring aspects of gourmet street food culture is the notion of the meet up. Whether officially sanctioned or more of a free for all, meet ups have continued on as a worthwhile way for small collections of trucks to band together and draw a larger crowd that all can enjoy. And in today's tougher market for gourmet food trucks, circling the wagons is exactly the right mentality.

Perhaps the most popular meet up in the entire city is also one of the oldest, and it goes down mostly on the first Friday of every month in Venice at the Brig, a casual drinking spot right along ultra-hip Abbot Kinney. Thanks to its large parking lot (an L.A. rarity, particularly in this neighborhood), the Brig has for years hosted an array of gourmet food trucks that share their eats with the nearby drinkers, shoppers and locals. It's where trucks like Kogi BBQ first got their real start, and the camaraderie among gourmet trucks continues there to this day.

One of the other most well-known destinations for consistently spotting gourmet food trucks is along Wilshire Boulevard, in what's known as the Miracle Mile. Though tensions have lessened considerably since the height of food trucks around 2010, there is still some lingering resentment from local brick-and-mortar restaurants who felt overshadowed or otherwise outnumbered by the influx of weekday gourmet trucks that would park along Wilshire, tempting the many officeworkers in the area at lunch time.

Parking enforcement issues and zoning rights quickly came into play, and for a while a standoff ensued, with local eateries harassing trucks as much as possible and vice versa. Since then, the herd of gourmet street food operators has naturally thinned, and there seems to be enough fast, casual lunchtime business to go around. Trucks still park in clusters every weekday along Wilshire Boulevard, between Fairfax Avenue and Hauser Boulevard, but without the chaos or overt

Dave Danhi of the Grilled Cheese Truck. *Elizabeth Daniels.*

competition. Officeworkers and neighborhood folks line up to try one truck one day, another truck the next. There's always something to enjoy from the dozen or so mobile vendors out front, with new trucks rotating in regularly.

And that's perhaps the biggest single upside for today's gourmet food truck customer: variability. Unlike more authentic, culturally driven vendors, chefs on board a gourmet truck are open and willing to switch up menus based on seasons or last-minute specials. There is also still a wider supply of gourmet trucks overall, so curious diners can enjoy snackable bites from a handful at once the next time they all congregate for a large block party or at designed truck meet ups.

For truck owners and chefs themselves, the upside to all of the headaches and long hours is a higher total payday than one of the cheaper loncheros around town, and with roughly the same overhead costs. The relationship to customers is also more compelling, since generally the person working the griddle or expediting dishes is the same one who signs the paychecks and drives the truck home at the end of a shift. Plus, success stories like Kogi BBQ seem to abound, making the dream seem close at hand—never mind that those stories are exceedingly hard to come by.

Here are some of the best, most enduring gourmet food trucks operating in Los Angeles.

THE STREET FOOD LANDSCAPE IN LOS ANGELES TODAY

KOGI BBQ

Open: midday and late night
Location: varies

The food truck that started a revolution. The fusion flavors that built an empire.

There is no way to overstate the importance of Kogi BBQ not only as a food option for the city but also as a stand-in for the sort of dining and cuisine changes that would take Los Angeles by storm in the coming years.

The brainchild of Roy Choi and co-founders Mark Manguera and Caroline Shin, Kogi BBQ elevated street food from a late-night desperation to a sought-after destination. Harnessing the early promise of Twitter as a social mobility platform, Choi and his roving team of Tweeters gained a following in part because of their elusiveness; Choi would pull "gangster stops" anywhere he felt like it, sometimes for thirty minutes and sometimes for hours, letting lines form as hungry diners raced across town in search of a meal.

The menu, a weighty blend of Korean and Mexican influences (the perfect blend for multicultural Los Angeles), remains largely unchanged

The blackjack quesadilla from Kogi BBQ. *Paul Bartunek.*

since those early days. Choi's short rib taco is still there and just as iconic, while loaded burritos and ultra-crispy quesadillas anchor options beyond the taco. There's a burger (and sliders) on the menu now, along with mulitas, tofu offerings and a spicy Sriracha bar for dessert, but the original order—three short rib tacos and a drink—is just as popular as ever.

The Grilled Cheese Truck

Open: midday and late night
Location: varies

Dave Danhi may not be a household name, but there's a good chance that you've heard of his gourmet operation, the Grilled Cheese Truck. It's a Los Angeles staple, though more recently the burgeoning company has gone national, setting up shop in several other states and selling public shares in an attempt to touch every corner of the country.

Danhi's concept of chef-driven grilled cheese sandwiches wasn't unheard of when he started up the Grilled Cheese Truck, but it was among the most thorough. Armed with a concept that was already being realized by other

The Grilled Cheese Truck. *Elizabeth Daniels.*

operators (both on trucks and inside brick-and-mortar restaurants), Danhi set about streamlining the process and seeking out maximum access to customers. Working everything from food festivals to late-night stops outside bars in Venice, the Grilled Cheese Truck soon gained a reliable reputation. Coupled with the gooey riffs being taken with the normally home-cooked sandwich, Danhi soon had a hit on his hands.

The truck's signature sandwich is the overloaded cheesy mac, a grilled cheese sandwich tucked with actual mac 'n' cheese (sharp cheddar, of course) and, if requested, BBQ pork. Dippable sides of tomato soup are always available, and anyone craving something sweet can find a small collection of dessert melts that offer takes on traditional apple pie and s'mores. As always, the success of the Grilled Cheese Truck remains its ability to be all things to all people.

DOGTOWN DOGS

Open: midday, evenings and late night
Locations: varies

Oddly enough, Los Angeles is not really a hot dog town. We have street carts serving bacon-wrapped versions outside Hollywood nightclubs, and there are touristy stops like Pink's Hot Dogs on La Brea, but all things considered, the taco rules here in a way that hot dogs never could.

Which makes it all the more intriguing that a simple little can-do operation like Dogtown Dogs can spend so many years on the streets, serving hot dogs to its mostly Westside clientele. Titled after the colloquial nickname for L.A.'s Venice neighborhood, Dogtown Dogs aims to marry the laid-back, coastal surfer vibe with quality ingredients at a price point that isn't out of this world.

The results shine through in the intriguing recipes, like the six-dollar Trailer Trash dog that dumps beef chili, nacho cheese and Frito's chips on top of the usual all-beef frank. The Morning Commute pins a fried egg to the top of a bacon-wrapped hot dog. Any of the slightly outlandish options can also be paired with a small side of tater tots or the more popular three-dollar Buffalo Tots, which soaks the tots in a fiery hot wing sauce beforehand. Simple? Yes. Effective? Absolutely.

GUERRILLA TACOS

Open: midday
Location: Wednesday at Cognoscenti Coffee in Culver City, Thursday and Friday at Blacktop Coffee in the Arts District downtown, Saturday and Sunday at Blue Bottle Coffee in the Arts District downtown

Chef Wes Avila managed to pull off a rare 360-degree spin with his street cart turned truck Guerrilla Tacos. The French-trained chef studied under Alain Ducasse in Paris and moved up the ranks of some of Los Angeles's most progressive kitchens before leaving the staid life of a gourmet kitchen for the thrills of street food service. His concept, a high-end taco cart that is just as focused on quality of ingredients and interactions with the local farmers' market as any restaurant in town, didn't take long to catch on.

The aptly named Guerrilla Tacos began as what amounted to one-day lunchtime pop-ups in front of a downtown Los Angeles coffee shop and then slowly expanded hours as demand grew and grew. Soon, a full truck was in the works, with a dedicated staff to match. The mobility gave Avila the ability to chart new courses and feed more communities but almost always in the daytime—and usually near a coffee shop.

Today, Guerrilla Tacos follows largely the same path, though the menu changes daily and is entirely reliant on what Chef Avila feels like cooking and can find at the farmers' market or from his industry contacts. It might

Guerrilla Tacos parked in the Arts District. *Farley Elliott.*

A plate of tacos from Guerrilla Tacos. *Farley Elliott.*

be a foie gras taco one day or a one-off tamal the next. Seafood is popular here, and plenty of days a fried egg drapes over what amounts to a breakfast taco, but there's one thing for certain within the circular life of Avila and his Guerrilla Tacos outfit: surprisingly, no two days are ever quite the same.

The Urban Oven

Open: midday and evenings
Location: varies

In a city often maligned for its lack of great pizza, the Urban Oven roams free. Forget oversized reheated slices from the local corner shop; this matte black mobile pizzamaker pushes out hand-tossed pizzas made to order.

At only nine inches across, the smallish pies are meant to be single serving (as in, one pizza per person) and may take a little while to arrive. That's because each pizza is fired inside a wood-burning oven that's actually a part of the truck itself! Pizzas burn exceedingly hot, helping the crust to rapidly rise and take form without becoming too dense or chewy. Ingredients range from prosciutto to fennel sausage to veal meatballs and Thai shrimp, and there's rarely a drop in quality among the disparate options. It's hard to imagine a more satisfying midday lunch break.

Soho Taco

Open: midday and evenings
Location: varies

The best part about Los Angeles's street taco scene is its variety. Regional Mexican specifications might determine ingredients, preparation and even location of a given type of taco, but just as many trucks choose to play by their own rules. That's the world where Soho Taco comes from.

Rather than offering a pan-cultural fusion experience like the Kogi BBQ truck or something similar, Soho Taco focuses on bringing the

The Soho Taco truck. *Paul Bartunek.*

A plate of tacos from the Soho Taco truck. *Paul Bartunek.*

street taco experience upmarket a little ways. That means individual tacos are more expensive than the one-dollar variety found on countless street corners in L.A., but the return is a higher-quality product that offers flavors not normally found on the streets.

At Soho Taco, handmade corn tortillas arrive in massive portions, with two or three plenty large enough to feed one person. They're loaded with refined versions of the sort of ingredients that may seem common: a pulled and marinated chicken, a smoky carne asada, a battered bite of shrimp.

But the real move to make when dining at Soho Taco is to head for the vegetarian items, where quality ingredients can really show off. Since most local taco operations offer little in the way of non-meat options, Soho Taco is given free rein to shine. Peppers and onions mix with griddled mushrooms to offer a bit of crunch, a touch of sweet and plenty of depth, while other meat-free options bring their own dynamics to the party. And best of all: the tacos at Soho Taco only get better with a dollop of terrific housemade salsa.

LOS ANGELES STREET FOOD

KOMODO TRUCK

Open: midday and evenings
Location: varies, with storefronts in Pico-Robertson and Venice

In the hurried early years of gourmet tacos trucks, simple fusion was king. Most of the time, the overlapping flavors had Asian or South Pacific elements, mixed with the ever-popular litany of portable Mexican street food dishes. New tacos arrived nonstop, with fresh (or, in many cases, rehashed) notions of what did or didn't belong on a tortilla. Pretty quickly, the trend got tired, and only the fittest of the bunch survived.

One such specimen is Komodo, a simple black truck emblazoned with the namesake lizard on its side in stark white. Branching out from the more straightforward Kogi BBQ mix of Korean flavors and Mexican finishes, Komodo sought quickly to bridge several Southeast Asian cuisines at once—while using French techniques from a Le Cordon Bleu chef in Pasadena. The interesting cocktail of ideas has more than worked: it has become a phenomenon.

Now with two dedicated storefronts and a truck that still roams the streets, Komodo can say with certainty that it not only survived the initial wave of gourmet fusion food trucks, but it has also thrived in the process, selling tacos that might in one moment marry seared steak and a southwestern corn salad or pitch a reduced version of Indonesian beef rendang against a draping of tomato-cucumber salad and fried shallots. There's always something interesting to discover on the Komodo truck, assuming you can catch it before it rolls off to another stop somewhere across town.

LUCKDISH CURRY

Open: midday and evenings
Location: varies

As a county, Los Angeles is awash in fantastic Japanese food options. There's sushi, of course, as well as some of the most exciting udon and ramen in the nation. Practically all of those Japanese options exist as brick-and-mortar restaurants exclusively, though, and many of those aren't even found in the city of Los Angeles. Instead, they anchor strip malls in the Valley and the South Bay, where a large Japanese population still resides.

THE STREET FOOD LANDSCAPE IN LOS ANGELES TODAY

All of those details help to frame the conversation about Luckdish Curry, the sleek Airstream trailer turned Japanese curry cart. As a quick primer: Japanese curry is not the same as Indian or Thai curry (though it was originally derived from the Indian variety); those tend to be thinner and spicier than its more northeasterly counterpart. Think of the Japanese version as something closer to gravy, a thickened, usually dark sauce that, instead of being laced with citrus like lime or bursting with heat from seeded peppers, is much more mellow and hearty. Served over rice, usually in accompaniment with a fried chicken or pork cutlet, Japanese curry is meant to satisfy during the surprisingly cold winter months there.

At Luckdish, the curry options fall somewhere on the spectrum between authentic and pure invention. Here, curry is less a standalone sauce then it is a conduit for proteins like white meat chicken. Draped over rice the way that large cheese curds in gravy might straddle a plate of fries, the Japanese curry at Luckdish is meant to be satisfying without being quite so simple. More outlandish takes like a chicken curry nacho or quesadilla plate play on the flavors of Los Angeles without losing the ultimate cuisine destination: the northern islands of Japan.

THE LOBOS TRUCK

Open: midday, evenings and late night
Location: varies

Unlike most food trucks in Los Angeles, particularly the more recent gourmet versions, the Lobos Truck makes no allusions to a particular cuisine. This is snack food done with a late-night sensibility in mind. If anything, the truck might earn a reputation for American comfort food, though it's a stretch to say that anyone grew up having his or her mother make overloaded trays of wachos (that's nachos, except replacing tortilla chips with waffle fries).

A relatively late-game addition to the food truck market, the Lobos Truck quickly earned a following for its overclocked options, which go heavy on the stick-to-your-ribs staples like bacon, cheese and fried eggs. Burgers are a must-try, of course, composed of either Angus or American Kobe patties that get the griddle treatment before being laid low with options as wide-ranging as garlic aioli, cheddar and guacamole. Veggie and chicken

Above: The Lobos Truck. *Courtesy the Lobos Truck.*

Below: Wings from the Lobos Truck. *Courtesy the Lobos Truck.*

breast burger options are also available, but don't expect them to skip on the upgraded toppings.

Beyond the burgers, there's an entire section of the menu devoted to those wachos, along with a self-styled mac 'n' cheese bar, which offers a variety of cheesy options made right on the truck. Improbably, the Lobos Truck serves both lunch and dinner at various stops across Los Angeles. The lunch is the insane one because it would seem impossible to get any more work done back at the office following a meal here.

COUSINS MAINE LOBSTER

Open: midday and evenings
Location: varies

Cousins Maine Lobster is one of Southern California's most successful food truck exports. The two-man team (Sabin Lomac and Jim Tselikis) behind the popular fresh seafood operation found a large following in part because of their time on the television celebrity investment show *Shark Tank*, which eventually landed them a cash deal with real estate investor Barbara Corcoran in 2013.

The Cousins Maine founders haven't let all of that television fame go to their head, though. They still hit the streets hard, with multiple trucks canvassing daily office parking lots, street vendor events and weekend festivals from Ventura to Orange County. Armed with a franchise agreement, Tselikis and Lomac now offer trucks in Houston, Texas, and Phoenix, Arizona, as well, with a dozen more cities planned for expansion.

So what's with all the hype? It starts with the lobster, flown in fresh from the southern Maine coast. New England–style mayonnaise lobster rolls form the backbone of what's possible on the Cousins Maine truck, though warm butter versions are available as well. From there, lobster and shrimp tacos are possible, as are lobster quesadillas, clam chowder and more. Finish with that most Maine of desserts: a Whoopie Pie.

LOS ANGELES STREET FOOD

COOLHAUS

Open: midday and evenings
Location: varies

While architecture and ice cream may not have much in common on the surface, the unusual pairing has certainly found a formidable home in Coolhaus, the sleek fleet of ice cream sandwich trucks that roams the streets. A popular dessert option in the mostly savory gourmet food truck landscape, Coolhaus has managed to expand quickly in the less than five years since it started. Trucks now run in Austin, New York and Dallas, in addition to the Los Angeles original (there's also a brick-and-mortar dessert shop in L.A.'s artsy Culver City neighborhood).

At its core, Coolhaus is a simple blending of quality handmade ice cream and inventive cookies, piled high into messy, delicious sandwiches. The menu is relatively straightforward but achieves the sort of form and function balance that any quality architect hopes for. Brown butter–candied bacon ice cream might be buoyed by a maple flapjack or potato chip and butterscotch cookie—the possibilities are endless and the decisions left up to the diner.

Some flavor combinations are more apparently appealing than others (there's an avocado Sriracha ice cream, for example), though everything here has its place. And for as good as those ice cream cookie sandwiches are, occasional ice cream options like affogatos (that's a scoop of ice cream over a hot espresso) and milkshakes make for an even more interesting array of options.

SOUTH PHILLY EXPERIENCE

Open: midday and evenings
Location: varies

There was a time, funnily enough, when Philly cheesesteak trucks rolled through the streets of Los Angeles in alarming numbers. Imitators spawned imitators until it was impossible to discern one from the other. Some of those options are off the road altogether now, while others have pushed their way into brick-and-mortar restaurants. The cheesesteak wars, it seems, have finally ended.

A beloved ice cream sandwich. *Farley Elliott.*

The biggest winner of the battle? South Philly Experience. Despite the clunky name and graffiti-on-brick wrap job of its truck, the South Philly Experience team has managed to persevere for the better part of five years, emerging as essentially the only legitimate cheesesteak experience left on the streets.

So what's the secret to South Philly's success? Most would swear that it's the attention to detail. South Philly doesn't do much of anything without it being a direct nod to the City of Brotherly Love—bread from Amoroso's in Philadelphia is flown in constantly, Cheez Whiz is still the topping of choice and Tastykakes continue to be the dessert option here. The rest is up to the crew, which has continued to hone its craft making fantastic lunchtime and late-night sandwich options, mostly for the Westside crowds.

BABY'S BADASS BURGERS

Open: midday and evenings
Location: varies

Yet another mobile success story to emerge from the first food truck revolution, Baby's Badass Burgers continues to skyrocket in popularity years after first launching. The concept is beguilingly simple: serve quality, freshly made hamburgers from the truck, with the added caveat that there are always a few beautiful women around, drawing attention.

That's the Babes side of the Baby's Badass Burgers equation, and it's a bit ingenious. Parking their hot pink truck next to some low-slung office building in the middle of the week, the Baby's team is able to get entire floors to roll out front for an afternoon burger and a bit of playful fun. The success of that simple notion has led to franchises in Las Vegas, Orange County, Austin and Jacksonville.

Of course, the meals have to be worthwhile as well, particularly at their exaggerated price point. Thankfully, they are. Half-pound ground Angus burgers are cooked to order and provide the base to any of the possible iterations on the menu, from the Hot Mama, which loads the sandwich with cream cheese–filled jalapeños, to the Bombshell, a stunt burger that swaps out the usual King's Hawaiian bun for a pair of slim bacon grilled cheese sandwiches. Let's just say, this isn't food for the calorie-counting set.

THE STREET FOOD LANDSCAPE IN LOS ANGELES TODAY

FREE RANGE LA

Open: morning and midday

Locations: Fairfax Avenue, between Waring and Willoughby Avenues during weekday breakfast; Monday, Wednesday, Thursday and Friday at Motor Avenue, between Palms Boulevard and Woodbine Street, for lunch; Tuesday at South Santa Fe Avenue, between East Seventh Street and Violet Street, for lunch

Fried chicken is a fantastic unifier. Juicy, brined and breaded birds exist in many cultures and in countless forms. At Free Range LA, the upscale farmers' market darling turned food truck extraordinaire, fried chicken acts as a central meeting place—for customers, workers and the menu itself.

What started as a weekend fried chicken sandwich pop-up at the high-end Melrose Place farmers' market in West Hollywood has gone on to become one of the city's best mobile breakfast options, riding in the wake of coffeehouse-parking trucks like Eggslut (which has since gone off the road in favor of a stall at the Grand Central Market). By capturing the breakfast crowd—a time notoriously slow for food trucks otherwise—Free Range LA has been able to ostensibly own the market. Of course, routinely posting drool-worthy photos to social media always helps.

The real following for Free Range LA, though, will always be that fried chicken sandwich. It's one of the best in town: a wide, juicy affair that comes laced with a creamy slaw and a few just-right slices of hot Fresno chiles. Of course, if breakfast is a must, there's always the popular breakfast burrito and the truck's signature homemade biscuits, which are meant to hold anything from tempura-fried, free-range chicken to thick slices of sizzling bacon. It's rare for a single truck to do two meals a day (let alone to do them well), but Free Range LA makes it all look easy.

Chapter 13
Food Halls and Markets

S ince the very inception of Los Angeles, willing businessmen and home cooks have opted to make a little extra cash by selling the sort of meals they were familiar with. But in wide-open L.A., which stretched from the ocean to the L.A. River downtown, often with little congestion in the middle, attracting a hungry crowd was not always possible.

To allay the potential for failure, clusters of like-minded vendors began huddling together at particular locations on particular days (or, in many cases, daily). By joining forces and working in manageable bunches on dedicated plots of land, a food cart's chances of attracting more overall customers (one interested in the array of choices or happy to know that the location and timing can always be relied on) increased dramatically.

Of course, this model is nothing new. Farmers' markets and open-air bazaars have been a necessary way of life for centuries and remain so in many parts of the world. They are vibrant, often crowded places where communities and outsiders alike can congregate over meals and purchase their necessary goods for the day, week or longer. In Mexico, plazas like the Zócalo public square have been acting as a semi-sacred gathering place since the Aztec times.

Today's open-air markets in Los Angeles are as thriving as ever. Following decades of languishing as a perceived second tier-dining option meant only for the occasional tourist or hard-up local, the city's food halls now command serious respect. And the food is better than ever.

LOS ANGELES STREET FOOD

OLVERA STREET

Open: 10:00 a.m. to 6:00 p.m. weekdays, 10:00 a.m. to 10:00 p.m. weekends
Location: 845 North Alameda Street, Los Angeles, CA 90012

Downtown's Olvera Street is more than just a cultural icon for the city of Los Angeles. It is history reincarnate, albeit with a more modern sensibility and an added bit of kitsch.

One of the city's oldest and most cherished gems, Olvera Street is an open-air mall, lined with brick and roughly a block long. It sits on some of the oldest real estate ever established for the city of Los Angeles and has a knack for calling itself L.A.'s very first street.

The pathway was first established more than two hundred years ago, situated in front of the Avila Adobe, which dates to 1818 and is the oldest standing residence in the city of Los Angeles. Over the years, it became a more modern thoroughfare (for the time, anyway), acting as the de facto center of town and thus sitting in as the setting for all manner of public transactions.

By the late 1800s, however, citywide expansion had made Olvera Street less important, and it became a haven for new immigrants to the city, eventually falling from there into a state of disrepair.

In the 1920s, a revitalization effort by the Sterling family once again brought prominence to Olvera Street by reimagining it as a closed-off pedestrian walkway, lined with shops and selling a version of "authentic"

A plate of taquitos. *Paul Bartunek.*

118

Mexican heritage. It's a colorful reinterpretation of the original Olvera Street, but one that still works today, as vendors line the center of the boulevard and small shops sit in a row along both sides, selling small toys, blankets, cowboy hats and, of course, food.

The primary dish found along Olvera Street is the taquito, a rolled corn tortilla that's stuffed with shredded meat and fried. Usually served with a thin avocado salsa and perhaps a wash of shredded cheese, nearly every food stall along the strip serves its own version.

Arguably the best version (and inarguably the first) comes from Cielito Lindo, a small stall situated at the opposite end of Olvera Street from the Historic Plaza. What started as a small collection of tables and a single food stand in 1934 has since become an indelible part of Los Angeles cuisine and culture. Those same rolled tacos can still be enjoyed today, using the original recipe from more than eighty years ago.

Taking a walk up and down Olvera Street, you'll see plenty of competitors today. Small restaurants with outdoor patios share space with tight walk-up stands and eateries that are little more than serving windows, each frying up taquitos to waiting tourists and the occasional local. There are other menu items available, of course, from the carne asada nachos made of waffle fries at Las Anitas to the handmade tortillas and piles of pork carnitas at La Luz Del Dia, which has been on site as a fully operating restaurant since 1959.

Though certainly touristy and lacking much of the modern-day street food experience, Olvera Street remains an important part of Los Angeles and an easy stop-off on any tour of downtown. Its location across the street from Union Station makes it easy to navigate, too, so if you're fresh off the last train or looking to enjoy a bite along downtown's oldest avenue, check it out.

GRAND CENTRAL MARKET

Open: 8:00 a.m. to 6:00 p.m. Sunday through Wednesday, 8:00 a.m. to 9:00 p.m. Thursday through Saturday
Location: 317 South Broadway, Los Angeles, CA 90013

There is no better example of the rejuvenation of the open-air market as a viable dining option than downtown's Grand Central Market. First opened in 1917, the thirty-thousand-square-foot space has been in continuous operation ever since, as the city exploded and expanded around it.

THE STREET FOOD LANDSCAPE IN LOS ANGELES TODAY

At its inception, the market was a haven for the rich, who occupied stately Victorian mansions atop Bunker Hill, which overlooked the smallish city. Servants and rich families willing to venture out for a stroll would take the adjacent funicular known as the Angels Flight down to the market to shop for the day's produce, flowers and any needed dry goods. Though the Angels Flight, which opened initially in 1901, is still there, it hasn't been operational since a safety incident in 2013.

Grand Central Market, on the other hand, is in the midst of its greatest years since opening. Its previous heyday may well have come in the 1940s and '50s, when the idea of routinely eating meals outside of the home as a form of enjoyment, coupled with the immediately massive growth of a Southern California fast-food culture, led to a blossoming of the market as a haven for upstart vendors.

In the decades that followed, the market began to lose its luster as a consumer mainstay, as the proliferation of cheap automobiles and suburban idylls dethroned any notion of a walkable urban core. Everyone flocked to the edges of town, venturing in only during work hours or on weekends to explore museums and one-off cultural attractions. The market languished.

After years of throwing off longtime tenants who could no longer hold on, Grand Central Market settled into a sort of soft stasis through the late 1980s and well into the 1990s. The clientele became almost exclusively working class and largely Hispanic, with central greengrocers updating their produce (and their prices) to survive in the changing market. Bargain-basement stalls soon proliferated, while many areas of the market simply remained empty.

Only the strong survived, like China Café and Tacos Tumbras a Tomas, a fan favorite taco shop. Both are still alive today and, along with the recent influx of new tenants, thriving.

The latest revamp of the longtime space, which will hit one hundred years old in 2017, began in earnest following a 2012 renovation. Positioning itself as a low-cost alternative for talented chefs in a wounded economy, Grand Central Market managed to revamp an underused patio and bring in a Texas-style barbecue operator while simultaneously turning an open corner of the interior

Stalls at Grand Central Market. *Farley Elliott.*

into arguably the city's best new coffee shop. Add in a former morning food truck turned breakfast counter and a neo-traditionalist Thai spot serving market-driven comfort food and a star was soon born.

Accolades galore have followed the rise of the market, including a spot on *Bon Appetit*'s 2014 list of the Best New Restaurants in America. Since then, flocks of food lovers, tourists and curious locals have been descending on the space, proving once and for all that if given enough time, what's old will inevitably become cool again.

Here are some of the best vendors currently operating inside of Grand Central Market.

Eggslut

A market darling since the beginning of Grand Central's new wave, Eggslut is the cheeky breakfast counter that everyone's still talking about. Thanks to its racy name and beautifully simple white subway tile décor—not to mention the insanely drool-worthy egg sandwiches—Eggslut has earned a spot as one of the most photographed restaurants in all of L.A. It also has one of the longest lines.

A breakfast sandwich from Eggslut at the Grand Central Market. *Farley Elliott.*

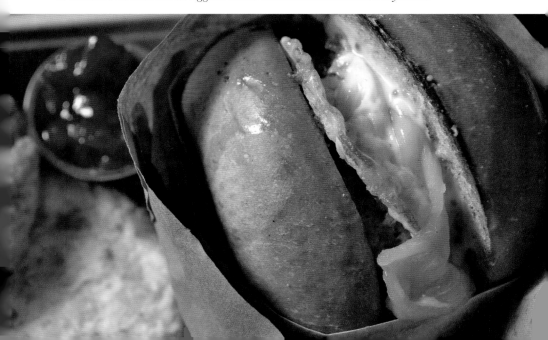

Yes, there will be lots of tourists waiting for the same breakfast sandwich as you. It's a function of the market's explosion in popularity, and Eggslut chef/co-owner Alvin Cailan's willingness to jump in front of a camera to re-create his morning masterpieces for magazines, TV shows and online publications. If your only option is a weekend maneuver, try to arrive early—Eggslut opens at 8:00 a.m. and closes at 4:00 p.m. daily.

But if you can, a weekday arrival is your best bet. The lines are shorter, the market a bit less crowded. Seats at the long, open counter that overlooks the grill can be had with a lot less pushing and shoving, and that's where you want to be if you can.

With an easy sightline, it's possible to spy the signature sandwiches and the griddled eggs that will form their base. A bacon, egg and cheese is as simple as they come, though the Fairfax (a mix of softly scrambled eggs, cheddar cheese, caramelized onions and sriracha mayo on a warm brioche) is one of the most popular orders. And then there's the namesake Slut, a coddled egg cooked in a glass jar over a potato purée. It's a reimagined meat-free breakfast plate, whipped up into silky perfection.

G&B Coffee

This walk-up coffee counter is deceivingly pedigreed; you'd have to seek out the two U.S. Barista Championship trophies tucked away atop one corner of the long chalkboard wall just to get a sense of the strength behind the operation. Those two trophies belong to Kyle Glanville and Charles Babinski (the G and the B, respectively), longtime specialty coffee veterans who began under the Intelligentsia banner and now own other well-respected shops in town.

The drinks served here, from high-end espresso options to pourovers, teas and even the occasional coffee milkshake, are all quite special. Rotating roasteries ensure a range of unique options for coffee aficionados, while the uninitiated can enjoy a simple black coffee poured by one of the nation's best.

Just don't expect to sit around and relax at G&B. A few stools line each side of the long, open counter, but they're in high demand. Instead, belly up to the standing bar anytime after 7:00 a.m. and enjoy a quick drink before moving on. The staff is no less friendly, and the feel of a small, intimate morning encounter before hustling off to the day's events is positively European. If you must stick around, weekly Wednesday coffee cuppings let curious coffee drinkers explore different roasteries and coffee styles in a concentrated, fun environment.

G&B Coffee at Grand Central Market. *Farley Elliott.*

Wexler's Deli

Los Angeles's strong Jewish deli tradition may have slowed down in recent years, but there's still really no comparing the scene here to any other American city—New York included. Longtime locations like Langer's Deli carry the traditional pastrami, corned beef and smoked fish banner proudly, while a new crop of intrepid deli masters is turning the corner toward a new generation.

Perhaps the best example of this in the city is Wexler's Deli, a clean walk-up counter right in the heart of the Grand Central Market, offering a strong daily variety of housemade smoked meats and fish. Run by namesake chef Micah Wexler, the blindingly white corner stall seats roughly a dozen, opening early for the bagel and lox crowd and usually selling out by its 4:00 p.m. last call.

So what's the order of the day at Wexler's? Just about anything, really, considering the chef's penchant for traditionalism and detail. There are simple morning egg sandwiches done on stellar seeded bagels or ten-dollar batches of smoked sturgeon and cream cheese. For lunch, classic preparations like the O.G., a pastrami on rye with mustard, satisfy the skeptical old-school crowd, while headier bites like the MacArthur Park (a nod to the iconic #19 sandwich at Langer's Deli not far away) combine pastrami, Swiss cheese,

Russian dressing and coleslaw on that same fantastic rye bread. Don't skip on the pickles, which are, naturally, made in house.

And when you're ready for dessert, simply head next door to McConnell's for some of the city's best ice cream.

Las Morelianas

In some ways, the timeline for Grand Central Market should be marked as B.R. and A.R.—Before Revitalization and After Revitalization. There are the post-2013 vendors, shiny and idealistic, serving a new crop of customers and bringing accolades to the market from national publications. And then there are the older vendors, adapting to a new sense of vibrancy while, in some cases, struggling to hold on in a sea of change. For the market as a whole, every day is a balance.

And then there are operators like Las Morelianas, who seem to effortlessly straddle the divide between old and new. At first blush, the Broadway-side market vendor seems to be in a far different league than its neighboring Eggslut. There is none of the shiny glitz, no long counter or photographable logo. Instead, Las Morelianas is as no frills as they come, with little more

A cazo of cooking pork at Grand Central Market. *Farley Elliott.*

than a small space for ordering and a wide-open kitchen, showing the team at work.

It's what they're working on that makes all the difference, though. This Michoacan-styled stall is, in true homage to its homeland, all about the carnitas. Wide cauldrons boil over with more than a dozen cuts of pork that are ready to be handed over, making them a true snout-to-tail purveyor.

Unsure of the cut for you or looking to branch out beyond the usual safe bites of shredded shoulder? Just ask for a sample, and the team will happily hand over a taste, wrapped inside a thin single tortilla. During slower moments, the guys working the cazos will even hand out the little bites to passersby as a sort of tastebud calling card.

Not that they need the advertisement. Lines frequently stretch for the nearly decade-old stand, with morning customers lining up patiently for takeaway taco plates or stuffed tortas. Some even come to buy by the pound in order to take the haul home and enjoy it with family.

In the midst of Grand Central Market's total overhaul, it's refreshing to see stalls like Las Morelianas remain as popular as ever and even draw in a new generation of diners in the process.

Sarita's Pupuseria

As the traditional Salvadorean street snack, pupusas occupy a longstanding position within the Los Angeles food lexicon. Wide, thick discs of masa are hand formed and stuffed with a variety of simple ingredients, from beans to cheese to lightly braised meats, and then griddled to a slightly crisped perfection. It's meant to be cheap, delicious and served piping hot, with limited ingredients inside so as not to overwhelm their construction and ensure an even griddling.

At Sarita's Pupuseria, the nearly fifteen-year-old market vendor, the wide, hot cooking area is lined day after day with impeccable pupusa rounds, toasting up at the edges and heating through in a matter of minutes. There are nearly a dozen different filling possibilities, from simple beans to cheese to thin shreds of pork or any combination therein. Loroco, a spear-shaped edible flower bud common to much of Mexico and Central America, is also popular at Sarita's; even when pickled, it delivers an herbaceous flavor that's hard to match in the States and pairs well with gooey cheese.

The wide berth of intriguing options means that nearby officeworkers and anyone after a quick, reasonably priced lunch can line up all week long and never experience the same dish twice. That's important for business, and it's a large part of what's helped keep customers coming back for so many years.

Of course, being one of the most flavorful stalls in all of the Grand Central Market certainly helps. Based on recipes from namesake owner Sara Clark, each handmade offering at Sarita's is better than the last, though the accompanying sides are nothing to forget, either. Fried plantains and a rotating selection of stews and meats certainly keep things interesting. But at the end of the day, it's all about the pupusas (don't skip on the provided curtido either, which is a sort of zippy Central American fermented cabbage slaw meant to accompany your next plate of pupusas).

The Original Farmers Market

Open: 9:00 a.m. to 9:00 p.m. Monday through Friday, 9:00 a.m. to 8:00 p.m. Saturday, 10:00 a.m. to 7:00 p.m. Sunday
Location: 6333 West Third Street, Los Angeles, CA 90036

Several miles away (though a small lifetime in Los Angeles traffic terms) from downtown's Grand Central Market is the Original Farmers Market, a sprawling food vendor complex butting up against the busy intersection of Fairfax and Third. Though not technically the oldest open-air market in town (that title, too, belongs to Grand Central, which first rolled up its doors in 1917), the Original Farmers Market is perhaps L.A.'s most recognizable.

With its iconic clock tower, wide parking lot and low-slung demeanor, the Original Farmers Market has stood across decades as a place for casual diners to stroll the aisles, snacking from whatever purveyor catches their fancy. It has been that way essentially since 1934, when the on-site landowners began allowing farmers, merchants and small restaurants to operate. As time rode on, the market gained prominence within the growing community and, by the 1950s, had earned a sense of cult status for the rapidly changing city.

Today, the Original Farmers Market has undergone its own level of revitalization, as it continues to manage the old and the new in equal measure. Much-beloved vendors still occupy their prime real estate inside, though a few local chef luminaries have over the years taken to grabbing a foothold in the tourist-heavy market.

Of course, adjacent shopping complex the Grove has certainly helped to fortify the Original Farmers Market legacy. A twenty-five-acre retail

Above: A vendor stall inside of the Original Farmers Market. *Courtesy Short Cake.*

Below: A food stall at the Original Farmers Market. *Paul Bartunek.*

complex first brought to life in the late 1990s but not completed until 2002, the Grove has become one of the foremost shopping destinations in all of L.A. It's one of the most trafficked areas in the city, with millions of tourists alone crowding the curated main thoroughfare and ducking into national retail chains.

The boost in foot traffic for the area has naturally spilled over into the Farmers Market, which is separated by nothing more than a small crosswalk. Crowds flow seamlessly from one to the other, experiencing the great joys of the more traditional market with the upscale decadence of L.A.'s most popular outdoor shopping mall.

Of course, it's still quite possible to skip all of the pomp of the nearby Grove in favor of the more relaxed market. Many folks from the surrounding neighborhoods do just that, sneaking in for a bite or to pick up a few last-minute produce items (or just hitting the Starbucks before heading off to work). There are even several small bars within the market, and drinking is allowed just about anywhere inside, making it a great post-work destination for a pitcher of beer with friends or a late-morning breakfast with a Bloody Mary kicker.

Plan your trip right, and it's possible to duck into the many stalls and walkways without ever noticing the increased commercial presence next door; close your eyes and listen closely, and you might find yourself back in the 1950s, grabbing a doughnut or scoop of ice cream from one of the local vendors still on site. You might even stumble across one of the longtime regulars, returning for a taste of nostalgia.

While there are even a few sit-down restaurants on site at the market these days, like Los Angeles breakfast legend Du-Par's (don't skip the pancakes), the best experiences are still had at the stalls. Here are a handful of the Original Farmers Market's best vendors, from the revered to the recent.

Loteria Grill

A full decade before the arrival of upscale chef Neal Fraser and his Fritzi Dog concept to the Farmers Market, there was Jimmy Shaw. The Mexico City–born chef opened his first (of now many) Loteria Grill concept right in the heart of the Original Farmers Market in 2002, serving authentic Mexican cuisine well before the city's more recent infatuation with the complex true flavors from our neighbor to the south.

Tacos from Loteria Grill at the Original Farmers Market. *Paul Bartunek*

Eschewing the Tex-Mex culture altogether, Shaw sought to cook uncompromisingly, leaning on the ingredients and recipes familiar to him in his native central and southern Mexico. That's largely the same priority at today's Loteria Grill, which also enjoys full sit-down restaurants in Hollywood, Santa Monica and beyond.

The menu at Loteria Grill is studded with classic Mexican dishes and chef's favorites, done with an upscaled turn despite the low-frills environment. Tacos, tostadas, sopes and burritos utilize hand-formed tortillas and come filled with braises and moles—a far cry from the more commonplace Northern Mexico–style grilled meats one might be accustomed to. Larger format specialties like chicken in mole sauce, chile rellenos and pork carnitas make for a full evening meal.

Like the rest of the Farmers Market, it's best not to expect too much when thinking of seating options at Loteria Grill. Though there is an area filled with metal patio tables and chairs meant for the use of Loteria customers, it's mostly still come-as-you-are seating, which means nabbing a table in proximity to the open kitchen can be a challenge on busy weekends. Still, the overall market is teeming with seating options up and down the aisles on both sides, so finding something shouldn't be an issue, even if you are navigating a full tray of delicious Mexican favorites as you scout for a seat.

THE STREET FOOD LANDSCAPE IN LOS ANGELES TODAY

Bob's Coffee and Doughnuts

It doesn't get much more classic than Bob's Coffee and Doughnuts, the shingled shack helping to hold down the eastern end of the Farmers Market. On site since 1947 and under the same current ownership since 1970, Bob's is practically synonymous with fresh, quality doughnuts in L.A.—no small feat considering the wealth of doughnuts in this town.

Every day, all day long, dozens of fresh varieties emerge from the open kitchen, ready to be finished with a quick hand and snatched up by customers even quicker. Though the stand keeps true bakers' hours (it opens daily at 6:00 a.m.), more often than not there'll be someone in line ahead of you, ready to take a dozen to their morning meeting or grab a quick sugary snack while walking around the market.

Bob's cake doughnuts number nearly two dozen, with everything from the dense, plain versions that are perfect for dunking in a cup of coffee to lighter buttermilk options and one-off varieties that use honey and wheat as a base. For kids, the Bob's team routinely crafts specialty doughnuts adhering to unique shapes, and on holidays there are entire rows devoted to colorful, playful confections. And definitely don't skip the year-round doughnut holes.

On the raised doughnut side, the hefty apple fritters and bear claws are perennial favorites, but generations of families have also fallen in love with Bob's beignets, wide rectangles with an airy texture and raked with powdered sugar. These may not satisfy purists who arrive straight from the halls of Café du Monde in New Orleans, but as standalone delicacies, they're virtually unrivaled.

Fritzi Dog

On the more recent end of the spectrum, there's Fritzi Dog, which to the untrained eye may seem to blend in seamlessly with the older vendors. But look closer at the hand-painted signage hanging over the stall and you'll realize pretty quickly that Fritzi is anything but your average hot dog stop.

Brought to life in 2012 by longtime Los Angeles chef Neal Fraser, Fritzi Dog is an antibiotic-free, nitrate-free, humanely raised hot dog house. Fraser and his team focus on using only prime cuts of meat, ensuring an upscale hot dog experience from the first bite on.

That's certainly not to say that the menu suffers as a result. At any given time, there are at least eight different hand-cased hot dog varieties on offer,

from beef and pork "ballpark" classics to spicy pork, jalapeño chicken, all beef and the rare poultry combination of turkey and duck. From there, links are customized to order, with more than two dozen options for toppings, ranging from the sloppy (beef chili, slaw) to the esoteric (cilantro lime dressing, avocado). Even the bun is hand picked, with a gluten-free option. Sides range from tater tots to garlic fries, though the cauliflower popcorn is a surprise that should not be overlooked.

What's better: Fritzi Dog's old school ethos and new school food model means that classic hot dog combinations can be subbed with either a corn dog or a vegan carrot dog, which, despite the odd notion, is actually rather tasty. The whole thing is cooked sous vide and laced with spices; it may never be a substitute for any real meat eater, but as an animal-free option at a hot dog stand, it's a surprisingly worthwhile alternative.

Gill's Old Fashioned Ice Cream

There's never been a bad time for ice cream in Los Angeles, thanks to the temperate year-round climate. It's one of the reasons that Gill's Old Fashioned Ice Cream has been able to anchor the Original Farmers Market for so long, and after all these decades, it shows no indications of slowing down.

Originally opened in 1937, just three years after the start of the market itself, Gill's remains a stellar example of family values and quality products, while much of the surrounding area has swelled with new life over the years. The shop is still family run and maintains a colorful, playful atmosphere that draws in new generations of dessert lovers every summer.

Current septuagenarian owner Bob Gill grew up at the market, following early in his father's footsteps. As a teenager, Gill would scoop ice cream for tourists and stay late to clean up the stall. In the early years, it was all simple flavors and waffle cones, but as the tastes of the customers advanced, so too did the offerings available on site.

It's no surprise, then, that Gill's Old Fashioned claims itself as an early innovator (or, at the least, early adopter) of such popular present-day flavors as Rocky Road and Rum Raisin. Fall further down the rumor mill, and you might even hear that Burt Baskin, one half of the famous Baskin-Robbins

Opposite: Hot dogs from Fritzi Dog. *Courtesy Fritzi Dog.*

ice cream chain, was an early fan of Gill's—eventually taking an off-hand comment about the number of flavors served at that Farmers Market stall and turning it into the well-known "31 Flavors" slogan.

In truth, Gill's has no need to rely on such history lessons in order to draw in customers. The ice cream is as flavorful as ever, and waiting lines still occasionally snake through the open alleyways of the market, forming in anticipation of their next fresh scoop, sundae, cone full of soft serve or milkshake.

Short Cake

A few years back, as the Farmers Market was working on a slow overhaul that would bring in new tenants (and a fresh crop of tourists and interested locals), word began to spread that local restaurateurs Bill Chait and Amy Pressman were looking to enhance the southwest corner of the market. Their concept, in partnership with James Beard Award–winning pastry chef and Osteria Mozza legend Nancy Silverton, was simple: offer fast, casual food using high-end ingredients.

Working off a playbook that Pressman and Silverton devised, Short Cake today relies on inventive ingredients and quality production to produce some of the best pure baked goods in Los Angeles. It should be no surprise; the famous female duo helped to reinvent a stagnant dessert pastry culture after landing on the opening team at the now-famous Wolfgang Puck restaurant Spago in Beverly Hills.

Through new overall pastry chef Ivan Marquez, Short Cake has yet again reinvented itself as a pastry house par excellence. Driving recipes with the sort of market-fresh attitude mostly reserved for full-service farm-to-table restaurants, Marquez is currently playing with the edge between modern and classic, using Old World techniques to deliver top-notch new desserts.

Of course, there is a savory side to the takeaway café, along with a coffee program designed by Verve Coffee Roasters out of Santa Cruz. Short Cake's diminutive location at the west end of the Original Farmers Market perhaps keeps it a bit under the radar, particularly for casual shoppers who meander over from the Grove looking for a quick, sweet bite. It's certainly not a vendor to be overlooked, though.

If you're interested in spending more than a passing few minutes at the Original Farmers Market (and you should, given its history and importance

An assortment of pastries from Short Cake at the Original Farmers Market. *Courtesy Short Cake.*

to Los Angeles's food movement), be sure to seek out Short Cake—if only for the beautiful display of delicacies.

El Mercado De Los Angeles

Open: 10:00 a.m. to 8:00 p.m. Monday through Thursday, 10:00 a.m. to 9:00
   p.m. Friday, 9:00 a.m. to 9:00 p.m. Saturday and Sunday
Location: 3425 East First Street, Los Angeles, CA 90063

Though far newer than both the Original Farmers Market and downtown's Grand Central Market, El Mercado de Los Angeles is no less fascinating as a casual market for anyone looking to browse through rows of artisanal and handmade products or—more importantly—eat extremely well.

Known locally as just El Mercadito, the three-story structure sits at the corner of East First Street and Lorena Street in Boyle Heights. The neighborhood, which for decades stood in as the culturally Jewish center of Los Angeles, has in more recent times become the acting heart and soul of Los Angeles's Mexican American community. Even as changes have rolled through the historic downtown-adjacent streets, Boyle Heights (and its very active citizens) remains fiercely independent, warding off attempts at over-development and unwanted commercialization, even as many surrounding (and historically Latino) neighborhoods have largely succumbed to the pressures of rising housing costs, mixed-use construction and newer demographics.

El Mercadito is, in some ways, a capsule of that same story. First brought to the neighborhood in the late 1960s by the Chayra family, the market was envisioned as a place for the bustling Mexican American community to congregate comfortably. It would mirror many of the local markets found in Mexico proper, complete with its wild array of vendors selling items large and small, along with on-site options for simple snacks and handmade treats, ranging from tacos and tamales on down.

Spanning three stories, El Mercadito quickly found its niche within the Boyle Heights community. Local vendors flooded the stalls, bringing with them their unique wares and penchant for salesmanship. Leather goods became a prominent staple at the market and remain as such today. Everything from cowboy boots to belts to cowboy hats can be purchased on site, along with the usual assortment of trinkets, toys and baubles. Norteño music blares over speakers, and the cramped walkways overflow with boxes of gifts or display cases of worthwhile food.

A fully stocked salsa bar. *Clay Larsen.*

THE STREET FOOD LANDSCAPE IN LOS ANGELES TODAY

It's always the food that keeps people coming back to El Mercadito. The market offers a true cross-section of Mexican food culture, particularly the sort of snacks usually found on street corners and in parks all across the country. Churros are near ubiquitous; fried up in large batches, they emerge warm and crunchy, dipped well in sugar but with a soft, steamy interior that makes for perfect snacky sweetness. Platano macho (fried banana) is another popular snack, relying mostly on its own caramelized sweetness to get the job done.

And then there are the tostilocos and dorilocos, bags of corn Tostitos or Doritos that have been split open on the sides and filled with all manner of extra ingredients. Peanuts are popular, as are many more neutral fruits and vegetables like cucumber and jicama. Add in a dash of citrus (lime juice, normally) and plenty of chile powder and eat the entire concoction with a fork straight out of the bag. For the more adventurous, consider adding cueritos, or pork rinds—it's an extremely popular street snack.

Should you need a more sit-down experience, there are small eateries lining the inside of the market, particularly near the entrance. Seating can be hard to come by, particularly for the meek and especially on weekends, but with a little luck and determination, a table can be had. Upstairs, a more refined dining experience is possible, complete with full dinner entrees and mariachi bands that play live, often dueling one another in friendly music competition, to the delight of the seated diners in the middle. While there, delight in the colorful wall murals, which tell the story of Mexico throughout history.

The largely cash-only market opens in the late morning every day and runs through 9:00 p.m. seven days a week. It is more than "family friendly." El Mercadito is built with children and adults alike in mind. Generations still come together to enjoy walking through the stalls, putting back toys that the children try to pick up and beg their mothers for or simply browsing the colorful collections with those freshly made churros in hand.

Don't be surprised if, walking along with the pulsing crowds, you end up spending more than you'd anticipated. Places like El Mercadito have a way of sneaking up on your wallet. And because these vendors are required to pay rent, prices tend to be just a hair higher than what you might find individually elsewhere. But that's exactly the point—El Mercadito has taken the best of a city full of individual vendors and helped to collect them in one place for easy perusal and maximum fun.

A lineup of waiting salsa. *Paul Bartunek.*

The Alameda Swap Meet and El Faro Plaza

Open: 10:00 a.m. to 7:00 p.m. daily
Location: 4501 South Alameda Street, Los Angeles, CA 90058

It is practically impossible to discuss the current overall state of Mexican food in Los Angeles (and, by large extension, street food as well) without turning attention to the Alameda Swap Meet in South L.A. It is perhaps the single best representation of the bustling market culture that exists south of the border. The Alameda Swap Meet is, in many ways, a bit of Mexico that has been transplanted right into the heart of Los Angeles County.

And you just can't talk about the Alameda Swap Meet without also mentioning El Faro Plaza, which is not only directly across the street but also a direct competitor that may well be doing things just a bit better than the original.

First, some backstory.

The Alameda Swap Meet is a decades-old institution in South Los Angeles. It sits in a heavily industrial, very tourist-unfriendly part of the city, south of the 10 freeway's cut through downtown and smack between the 110 and 710 freeways. Getting there requires not only a car but also plenty of patience and more than a few glances at the mapping app on your mobile phone.

THE STREET FOOD LANDSCAPE IN LOS ANGELES TODAY

Mostly composed of loading docks, refrigeration warehouses, machine shops and the occasional fast-food chain, the streets surrounding the Alameda Swap Meet can barely be considered a true neighborhood at all. For the better part of a century, the area has been used as an industrial outpost, for everything from auto manufacturing to aerospace, and today is no different.

While the Alameda Swap Meet is technically on unincorporated territory overseen by Los Angeles County (the area does not have its own mayor, for example), the nearby small industrial city of Vernon lies just across Alameda Street and counts fewer than 150 full-time residents in the annual census, meaning that even for a major metropolitan area like Los Angeles, this is no-man's land.

Overall, the area has improved greatly since the 1990s, when high crime plagued it, even during daylight hours. Today, the rejuvenated Swap Meet and overall rise in local prosperity have helped to push back much of the unseemly shadows that hung over Vernon and the surrounding streets, making the Swap Meet and adjacent plaza once again a popular weekend destination for Mexican and Central American families. Depending on your own level of comfort, this part of town can either still seem a bit sketchy or be absolutely full of excitement, so don't forget to pack your common sense (and a sense of adventure) when making the trek. You certainly won't be alone.

Most Saturdays and Sundays, lines of cars spill out from the side streets around El Faro Plaza and the Alameda Swap Meet, backing up into oncoming traffic for sometimes half a mile. The one-block stretch of East Forty-fifth Street comes alive with revelers, families and in-the-know tourists looking for a very distinct, "only in L.A." kind of experience. Weekdays are, of course, more relaxed (the Swap Meet is open every day except Tuesday).

On the south side of the street is the Alameda Swap Meet proper, a massively long warehouse building with a wide-open asphalt area at the front that is ringed by yellow gating. Most days, Mexican flags hang from the fence, blowing in the wind almost as a way to mark the territory, though the market itself could not be more accommodating to one and all. It is possible that, without knowing a few key phrases, there could be a bit of a language barrier—particularly during transactions for products or food—but that's the only real trouble you're likely to encounter, and it's a problem that is often easily sorted. Cash is king, as the saying goes, and offering payment with a genuine smile at the ready is more than enough to settle any possible miscommunications.

A plate of street tacos. *Paul Bartunek.*

The best thing to do when trying to tackle the Alameda Swap Meet is to just dive in anyway. There is too much to see, too much to do and too many people to do things any other way.

Outside, cumbia and norteño music blasts from a live stage, where performers belt their tunes to swaying families and couples. During more upbeat songs, expect to see plenty of line dancing and tightly choreographed moves from dance partners, as they twirl and whip in time to the music, all under the warm sun. At the fringes of the dance circle, vendors already begin to encroach, selling trinkets, drinks and snacks.

Inside the Swap Meet's main building, it's a similar free for all. Competing salesmen vie for the attention of the crowds, while others hang back, letting the customers come to them. While there's plenty of overlap in the products being sold or the services touted, the sheer wealth of options means that (improbably) there's room enough for everyone. Need to get your hair cut or nails painted? There's a stall for that. Want photos printed in thirty minutes flat? You can find it here, alongside a hardware stall, a stand selling T-shirts and not far from a row of mannequin heads donning pristine luchador masks.

The biggest on-site competition comes from the food. Many eateries line the walls of the Swap Meet, enjoying a fair bit of space as a fully built-out stall, complete with a few stools and an open kitchen. They're lined up side by side in places, making them seem to the untrained eye as a bit of a homogenous blur. Still others sit nearby in food trucks or operate out of small carts, creating a wonderland of possibilities.

Don't be fooled by the overwhelming supply of Mexican food here—each vendor has its strengths and weaknesses and relies heavily on a certain area of cultural influence when creating its menu. Chorizo from the Mexican city of Toluca could be the order of the day at one stop, while an adjacent vendor sells seafood indicative of the coastal Mexican state of Nayarit. Flautas are everywhere, as are churros, tortas and tacos. The only issue, it seems, is picking your favorite.

Among the endless vendors, it's possible to stumble over more than a dozen unique and interesting takes on Mexican cuisine, with more than a few Central American classic dishes thrown in for good measure. Don't be afraid of the variety or of trying things you might not be familiar with. When in doubt, just ask what the person in front of you got and order the same thing—it's hard to go wrong here and very easy to get things right.

And then, just like thousands of weekend customers before and after, you head across the street to El Faro Plaza. It's much newer than the Alameda Swap Meet, having come about only around 1989 before promptly being shut down by L.A. County officials for lack of permitting. It reemerged not long after and today enjoys a symbiotic, if slightly antagonistic, relationship with its more well-known cousin across the street.

The secret to El Faro Plaza, however, might just be the eats. While an insane number of vendors of all stripes hawk their goods over at the Alameda Swap Meet (including, yes, plenty of street food), El Faro Plaza is much more of a connoisseur's space. Offering a bit more breathing room (but not much), this indoor-outdoor plaza is nearly ringed with stalls selling Mexican food that is, in most cases, of a decidedly higher quality.

Not that the Alameda Swap Meet is bad—far from it. There is almost no other place like it in Los Angeles, and it can't be denied as a single-source destination for an incredible amount of Mexican food variety. But at El Faro, the things the vendors do, they do extremely well.

A busy open-air market table. *Paul Bartunek.*

Tacos de canasta is one unique option. Known as a basket or "sweaty" taco, these simple steamed delights tend to be filled with a simple bit of pork or mash of potato and chorizo and then steamed through completely. The result is a moist plate of softened tacos (they're often small and, as such, are sold by the dozen for a few dollars) and are at their height when drizzled with a bit of fiery salsa.

Another dish that is all too often underrepresented on Mexican food menus is the tlacoyo, a pre-Hispanic meal made by taking uncooked masa (the mixture used to make tortillas) and filling it with a simple bean filling, normally. The whole thing is griddled until just firm enough, with a few toasted spots and a soft, steam-set interior. Often made out of blue corn masa and served with salsa, it's a filling bite that is at the heart of Mexico itself and found easily at El Faro Plaza.

THE STREET FOOD LANDSCAPE IN LOS ANGELES TODAY

MERCADO OLYMPIC

Open: midday on weekends
Location: Olympic Boulevard at Central Ave., downtown Los Angeles

For an experience that balances the ease of use at places like Grand Central Market and the Original Farmers Market with the authenticity and occasionally overwhelming feeling of a place like the Alameda Swap Meet, there is always the Mercado Olympic.

Well known in certain circles but relatively undiscovered by the larger population of Los Angeles (especially surprising, given its location in rapidly growing downtown), the Mercado Olympic is on the one hand nothing more than a loose, informal grouping of dozens of weekend vendors. On Saturdays and Sundays, they line the sidewalks along Olympic Boulevard, just west of Central Avenue in what's known colloquially as the piñata district thanks to the many warehouses stuffed with Mexican candies, party supplies and, well, piñatas.

But on the other hand, the Mercado Olympic is something much more. It's a family-friendly weekend gateway to anyone who is serious about embracing the flavors of modern-day Mexican culture.

Making churros at the Mercado Olympic. *Paul Bartunek.*

Though it's a far cry from places like the Alameda Swap Meet, with its sensory overloading experiences and endless vendors, the Mercado Olympic isn't for beginners, either. There is no hand holding here and no credit cards taken; arrive early, bring cash and expect to have a great, immersive time.

To start off, park near the intersection of Olympic Boulevard and Central Avenue, then make your way west down Olympic until the market seems to thin out on its own. Duck into warehouses at your leisure or simply browse the vast array of items kept in large bins right on or next to the stuffed sidewalk. Woven blankets come in any color imaginable. Low-grade kitchen tools can be had for a song. Pore through piles of candy, dried chiles, spices and whatever else catches your fancy, and don't be afraid to ask what the prices are—there's a good chance they vary, depending on how intent you seem on buying.

When you're hungry, simply look around in any direction. Under shading tarpaulins and patio umbrellas, endless options await. There is a man making fresh churros next to a parked van, using a wide vat of oil and a mixing tool for the batter that looks more suited to masonry work. Wide griddles hold hot pupusas, quesadillas and sopes at the edges, waiting to be snatched up. Bacon-wrapped hot dogs are just as popular, sizzling away in their own juices before being slipped into a bun and run over with griddled onions and peppers. Plantains, cooked until soft and oozing sweetness, lie in deep trays.

Quesadillas are a particular phenomenon at the market. Many vendors serve them, hand patting the masa into the thick oblong shape more common to Mexico than America, where the thin tortilla half-moon quesadilla seems the platonic ideal. These are no worse for their differences, though, arriving stuffed with squash blossom or a mixture called huitlacoche, a funky corn smut reminiscent of truffles. Perhaps cheese is all you need or a smear of beans. That's fine, too; all you've got to do is ask.

There's plenty of elote to be had as well. The Mexican corn on the cob makes for a rich snack once its been grilled to perfection and smeared with mayonnaise, a bit of Parkay and plenty of salt, chile seasoning and usually a squeeze of lime. Prefer a less unwieldy snack? Get your corn to go by ordering esquites, which is a similar dish that more or less combines the same ingredients into a Styrofoam cup for simple on-the-go action.

Keep walking, snacking as you go, and you'll discover men frying up long sheets of fresh chicharrones, or fried pork skin. You might see a few Tolucan vendors selling their best green link chorizo or the occasional pescado man at the far end of the market who fries up thin strips of tilapia for an amazing homemade version of fish sticks. Forget tartar sauce; these are served with a squirt of hot salsa and a fork.

In the middle of the market, you'll find that the space opens up a bit, allowing for a bit of depth and some fresh air (all those cooks mean things can get a bit smoky). If you're intrigued by the slowly spinning stack of marinating pork al pastor nearby—and you really should be—then head to the back corner and order up with the men in charge. Take your ticket back to the man watching the meat cook, and he'll finish off the transaction with an unbelievable plate of smoky, delicate tacos.

Just across the open space you'll find carnitas instead, cooked in hot vats of lard until crusty on the outside and wonderfully tender within. Buy by the pound to take home for later or have the workers chunk off a few bites to slide into a taco; either way is the right way here.

Unofficially, the Mercado Olympic runs Saturdays and Sundays from 9:00 a.m. to around 5:00 p.m. It's important to remember that this is simply a collection of individual vendors, however, so hours may vary, people may not show up and food may run out earlier than expected. It's all part of the charm with the Mercado Olympic.

Chapter 14
Food Festivals

Another great option for curious eaters looking to enjoy a wide array of street food in a short amount of time is the food festival. The idea is a simple one: congregate all manner of cheap street eats in one location and charge an admission fee for the right to dine on their wares. It's also proved to be an ingenious way for vendors to build notoriety and for festival operators to (hopefully) make a little bit of money.

There are now dozens of food festivals every year in Los Angeles, catering to both high-brow chefs and street food vendors, or working within a specific cuisine range to offer a more curated food experience. While only a few specifically bill themselves as street food festivals, almost every event in town offers at least a passing glance at the experience. Often times, it's the Highland Park tostada maker pushed right up against a tent hosting the renowned chef with the big-name downtown restaurant. In any other city it might be a stark contrast, but the quality and quantity of L.A.'s street food makes it a common occurrence. There's even a good chance the tostada maker and top chef are already friends.

For customers, the upside to all of these festivals is, of course, the convenience. Rather than seeking out individual vendors all across the city, each with his own hours of operation and limitations, festival managers curate the day's lineup in advance. Often there are one or two (or more) big-name players in the street food scene signed on for the day, which helps to draw in their own adoring fans while also giving newcomers the opportunity to enjoy their offerings for the first time.

The line for ramen burgers at 626 Night Market downtown. *Noam Bleiweiss.*

Many of these festivals also do a great job of adding in smaller up-and-coming vendors, as well as cooks and chefs who may not normally be available at all—either because they generally ply their trade far out of town in places like Tijuana and Ensenada or because the people doing the festival cooking actually hold other jobs, be it a day job or line work in someone else's kitchen. Festivals like these shine a wider light on possibilities for street food beyond what's already close at hand by showcasing talent that might not otherwise get the opportunity for a larger stage.

Better still for customers or anyone traveling through and on a tight timeline, these festivals have the added bonus of being well scheduled. With just a bit of advanced planning, it's possible to plan a trip or a few days' getaway around a food festival, ensuring maximum street food return in the shortest amount of time.

There are a few obvious downsides, though. First, the cost: because of the wide swath of vendors on site at any given festival, overall costs per person can be prohibitive so that every vendor can share in the profit pool. Whereas a stop at one or two street food destinations could run up a tab of twenty dollars or less, festivals usually price down to only about thirty-five dollars at minimum and often cost much, much more. Then there are the practical limitations for festivalgoers. Trying to "eat to your value" is a common problem, where attendees spend their time trying to pack in as many vendor stops as possible rather than enjoying the day at a leisurely pace. It's also hard, frankly speaking, to eat so much in one sitting, no matter how delicious or unique the experiences may be.

And, of course, the lines. Because of the condensed nature of festivals and their once-a-year cycle, most end up being overpopulated with like-minded diners, which can lead to exceedingly long lines at the best vendors—or any vendors at all, depending on how many people show up.

All that aside, there is little substitution for the pure volume of street food that becomes possible with a food festival and the ease of use for anyone attending. It all usually combines to make for a great single-day experience, where eaters can try the sorts of places they've only ever read about without falling too far out of their comfort zone.

Here are a few of the city's best street food–leaning annual food festivals.

L.A. Street Food Festival

When: mid-summer

As the granddaddy of them all, the massive annual food party known as the L.A. Street Food Festival enjoys a place in the pantheon of amazing street food experiences in L.A. Now more than half a decade old, the outsized event has grown to include dozens upon dozens of vendors who line the Rose Bowl in Pasadena for a full day of serving crowds that number in the thousands.

The summertime event certainly never lacks for suitors, both on the vendor and the customer side. Despite the heat that often accompanies the outdoor affair, plenty of people are willing to make the trek to Pasadena to eat, serve and examine the state of Los Angeles street food through a festival lens.

For the vendors in particular, the L.A. Street Food Festival is seen as a steal. Unlike most promotional tasting events, this annual affair does not charge vendors for the right to serve their food on site. In fact, it heavily subsidizes many of the cooks and kitchens who come out, particularly those with less of an existing footprint in the L.A. street food scene. The policy has allowed the festival to grow massively in just a few short years; simply put, everyone wants to get in on the action.

It's easy to understand why. There is perhaps no greater single collection of street food bigwigs than at the annual Street Food Festival. You'll often find heavyweights like Mariscos Jalisco, the Boyle Heights fried shrimp taco truck

Cooking inside the Super Tortas D.F. truck in South L.A. *Julia A. Reed.*

often seen as the maker of the best single taco in all of LA. Al pastor kings Tacos Leo might make the rounds, along with a handful of Japanese takoyaki makers, San Gabriel Valley meat skewer cooks, ceviche makers and more.

Even full restaurants and high-end chefs are getting in on the action, using the popular event as a showcase for their brick-and-mortar concepts or to show off their range by prepping a dish that would otherwise be seen as out of their comfort zone. Usually, these places tend to already have a street food ethos (a breakfast taco spot, say, or a takeout burger counter), even if they technically operate indoors, but not always.

In years past, the L.A. Street Food Festival has included many of the best trucks, trailers, carts and gourmet food operators in town, from famous options like the Grilled Cheese Truck to Luckdish Curry, which serves Japanese-style curry dishes out of a retrofitted Airstream trailer. German sausage makers Currywurst are fans of the festival, as are places like the James Beard Award–winning Oaxacan restaurant Guelaguetza, which operates a restaurant in Koreatown.

And there's always room for the out-of-town crowd, particularly from south of the border. Baja seafood professionals like Mariscos el Mazateño and La Guerrerense have become unlikely staples at street food events like this in the past.

THE STREET FOOD LANDSCAPE IN LOS ANGELES TODAY

With tickets priced north of fifty dollars, some customers might see the L.A. Street Food Festival as too much money for too much hassle. And while it's certainly true that the warm summer weather, long lines and massive crowds (festival organizers have taken recently to capping tickets to five thousand customers, with no day-of sales) can conspire to make the festival seem sweltering, there's no denying the strength of the event. There's a reason it's one of the most popular annual food festivals in Los Angeles: because its also one of the best.

TACOLANDIA

When: early summer

A relative newcomer to the food festival circuit, Tacolandia has quickly garnered a reputation as the festival for anyone who's serious about his street food. Relying almost exclusively on its namesake taco as the food staple of the day, Tacolandia has grown into an annual behemoth that highlights the best of what Los Angeles has to offer.

The early summer session is put on by local alt-weekly publication *LA Weekly* and curated by noted street food writer Bill Esparza (the same man who penned the foreword to this book). Esparza himself does much of the legwork in recruiting names for the event, ensuring a healthy swath of previously unknown vendors and popular names alike.

The format of the festival is largely the same as most others: entrance tickets are sold in advance of the event, with vendors seeking refuge from the sun and the long lines under tented work stations clustered into groups. Customers line up early for the chance to avoid the longer lines (VIP tickets can also be purchased, giving easier access and longer hours to those willing to pay) and flood in once the hour strikes. Queues form and lengthen at many of the most popular stalls, but mostly everyone gets slammed with customers regardless. That's especially true for vendors who don't or can't pre-plate small portions of their menus for waiting customers. Cooking to order at events like Tacolandia is a death sentence and a surefire way to anger the hungry hordes.

Mostly it's a relatively relaxed, fun time at Tacolandia. Because the focus of the event is so specific, everyone there shares a common bond. Conversations happen easily among strangers, especially as the day wears

Crowds at the annual Tacolandia food festival. *Paul Bartunek.*

on and comparisons among vendors crop up. Friendly arguments play out, and discussions are had, but for the most part everyone is there to enjoy Los Angeles's most well-known street food.

Enjoy they do. With many dozen vendors on hand—including some selling taco-adjacent dishes like tostadas and ceviches, plus drinks, premade goods and desserts—there is always something interesting to try. Mix that vibe with a few must-eat vendors like the taco truck Carnitas El Momo or the Watts quesadilla maker All Flavor No Grease, and it's easy to imagine having a great time downtown, eating tacos with a few thousand new friends.

Though the lineup does change annually, there are always a few quality names atop the vendor lists at Tacolandia. La Guerrerense, the Baja-based mariscos stand, is a popular option, as is Wes Avila's reimagined lonchero Guerrilla Tacos, which parks daily in front of coffee shops around town. Authentic barbacoa makers Aqui Es Texcoco and Yucatanean restaurant Chichén Itza stick to the traditional methods, while Modern Mexican champions like Corazon y Miel, Bizarra Capital, Pez Cantina and even Kogi BBQ help to raise the Mexican-American flag high.

As in years past, there has also been a designated drinking space on site. With the proper wristband, guests can down craft beer and specialty drinks, along with a handpicked selection of tequilas. It's a great lubrication for the event and certainly ensures a fun time for those who partake.

The annual Tacolandia street food festival usually takes place in early to mid-summer and is located at downtown's historic El Pueblo plaza, adjacent to L.A. cultural icon (itself a street food mecca, of sorts) Olvera Street. For just over thirty-five dollars, guests can get access to roughly eighty of the finest taco makers in and around Los Angeles for a single afternoon. That's more than "not bad"—it's incredible.

626 NIGHT MARKETS

When: year-round

Taking a slightly different tack than both the L.A. Street Food Fest and Tacolandia, the burgeoning 626 Night Market brand trades Mexican street food heritage for a taste of Asia. Not only are outdoor bazaars and street markets extensively popular throughout the Asian continent, but they also tend to be among the best places to eat well in a respective city.

For generations, the most popular of these markets have occurred at night, when daytime produce vendors pack up and leave, making room for late-night hawkers to fill the space with their own equipment, selling whatever delicious meal they're most known for.

Unlike many street vendors in, say, Los Angeles, night market hawkers in Asia tend to offer only one dish and many times only one version of that dish. You get your meal the chef's way or you move on down the (endless) line. Even at focused street food operations like Tacos Los Güichos in Los Angeles, known for having some of the city's best pork carnitas, you'll find other options on the menu to choose from. Not at your friendly neighborhood Bangkok hawker market.

Much of this ethos has carried over to Los Angeles's own 626 Night Markets, which began several years ago in Pasadena. The numerical name refers to the phone area code for most of the San Gabriel Valley, which is home to millions of Chinese, Japanese, Filipino, Burmese, Vietnamese and Koreans. The San Gabriel Valley is the cultural core for anyone with Asian heritage living in or exploring Los Angeles, and for millions more it's become symbolic as a place to experience new perspectives—while eating amazingly well, of course.

Above: Takoyaki balls at 626 Night Market downtown. *Noam Bleiweiss*.

Below: A ramen burger at 626 Night Market. *Noam Bleiweiss*.

THE STREET FOOD LANDSCAPE IN LOS ANGELES TODAY

Playing on both the culture and the cuisine, the first 626 Night Market billed itself as an Asian-focused event, bringing unbridled flavors from the region to this smallish upper-class suburb of L.A. The marketing worked, and that first night market proved so successful that it was almost its own undoing. Customers waded through impenetrable crowds to try to make it to a vendor, any vendor, but found the crush of people who had come out with the same notion as them to be too overwhelming. Complaints were lodged, bad Yelp reviews given and the first 626 Night Market was almost the last.

Thankfully, the founders of the night market idea regrouped and reemerged in short order, promising (and delivering) to modify the event in order to make it safe and fun for all. Since then, the 626 Night Market brand has blossomed, adding a DTLA Night Market (that's DownTown Los Angeles), as well as an Orange County Night Market. The latter is held over two weekends in late spring/early summer in Costa Mesa and has been its own resounding success, drawing in curious diners who may not be willing or able to otherwise take the hour-plus trek to Los Angeles just for a food festival.

The budding downtown version of the festival, which launched in 2014 and now runs annually during the summer, cleared up many of the initial problems that plagued the festival. A wide berth inside a parking lot across the street from Staples Center helped to keep things orderly (only the line for the Ramen Burger truly got out of hand), and with an incredible amount of total vendors on hand, it seemed that almost everyone who came to eat could do so without much waiting at all.

As for the original 626 Night Market concept, that's still alive and well out in the San Gabriel Valley. Much like the L.A. Street Food Fest, the night market team quickly spread its wings into much bigger digs: Santa Anita Park, home to horse racing and summertime concerts. Now sporting over 160 vendors with every festival night it puts on, 626 Night Market has become its own massive festival beast, and it's still unlike anything else going at the moment.

Forget tacos or sandwiches or upscale restaurant entrees; the menu at 626 Night Market is so comprehensive, so mind-bogglingly large and diverse, there's practically guaranteed to be dishes you've simply never even heard of before. All the better for you.

At first you'll spot a bowl of ramen or cumin-laced meat skewers. Then you'll angle toward a fusion fried chicken sandwich or some fried takoyaki balls. Nothing out of the ordinary yet. And then, within the massive sprawl of the festival, you'll inevitably stumble onto whole grilled baby squid, stuck through with a stick and ready for portable eating. You might see whole fried potatoes, spiraled out into one long, thin, crispy wave, available to be snacked on. The Japadog tent will hit you next, splashing all manner of Japanese ingredients on top of its all-beef franks.

Boba is everywhere, there are cocktails made out of entire pineapples and somewhere deep within the tented recesses you'll find dessert. While searching, expect to see half a dozen other items you're unfamiliar with. That's what makes not only the 626 Night Market so incredible but also the entire 626 area code: it will always surprise and delight you, especially with its food.

Chapter 15
Farmers' Markets

I n recent years, farmers' markets have come to help redefine the way that all Angelenos think about their food, particularly where it comes from. Markets now exist as a fully viable alternative to traditional grocery shopping in Los Angeles; locals can lean on their local market's weekly ingredients to build a litany of fresh recipes for themselves and their family, without ever having to rely on packaged or processed meals again. And with the overall rise of available markets in all corners of the county, it's never been easier to swing through for a last-minute produce pick-up to help round out that midweek dish.

Even the restaurants in Los Angeles take careful notice of the markets. Chefs from the city's favorite eateries routinely arrive in droves at the Wednesday and Saturday Santa Monica Farmers Market, talking with buyers, farmers and growers of all types as the early morning fog lifts to show the coastline only a few hundred feet away. Still others may choose to take to their local farmers' market, be it in Hollywood, Malibu or Compton, snatching up crates of produce likely grown within two hundred miles of where they're standing. In L.A., farmers' markets are big business, for vendors and customers alike.

They also do more than just sell the bounty from local farmers. These markets have a serious street food element to them, from urban artisans selling their freshly baked baguettes (meant, in a very European way, to be taken away to a park somewhere with a side of cheese, butter and meat and devoured on the spot) to hot dish vendors who prepare entire morning,

Neil Strawder of Bigmista's. *Farley Elliott.*

lunch or evening meals that can be eaten right at the market or saved for later. Tamales, hot dogs, barbecue, pupusas, chili, salads, sandwiches, burritos—depending on the food you're craving, there's probably a farmers' market vendor in town that serves it.

Below are some of the best markets for eating well.

Santa Monica Farmers Market

Open: 8:30 a.m. to 1:30 p.m. Wednesday and 8:30 a.m. to 1:00 p.m. Saturday, both on Arizona Avenue, and 9:30 a.m. to 1:00 p.m. Sunday inside Heritage Square off Main Street

Not only is the Santa Monica Farmers Market widely considered to be the best possible place to buy fresh, organic local produce, but it's also a beautiful location for eating really, really well.

THE STREET FOOD LANDSCAPE IN LOS ANGELES TODAY

As noted above, the Wednesday and Saturday markets on Arizona Avenue have become the de facto place for local kitchens to replenish their weekly supplies, while a Sunday Santa Monica Farmers Market on Main Street serves a quieter local clientele. Throughout them all, the farmers and growers are the celebrities, with keen-eyed locals, wandering food writers, upmarket home cooks and executive chefs all vying for a bit of elbow rubbing with the men and women who grow their fruits, vegetables, nuts and grains. It's quite a sight.

Still, all that attention must mean that the market is doing something right. And indeed it is; waitlists just to earn a space at the twice-weekly produce party can drag on interminably. The wait seems worth it, though, given the ten thousand or so Wednesday shoppers who make the trek to Santa Monica every week. Those are pretty impressive numbers for a market that's been operating on site for nearly thirty-five years.

So what do all those thousands of browsers want to do besides squeeze melons and haggle over prices? Eat, of course.

Like most farmers' markets, there is the usual collection of tented vendors selling whatever they've made that day, from fresh-pressed juices to entire breakfast plates. Dishes that don't require much prep are popular, like freshly shucked oysters, salads and drinks. And because the crowd is understandably discerning, there's no skimping on quality or technique with the food for sale.

Still other vendors swing the other way, either prepping well in advance or cooking on the spot to the delight of passersby. Pastries from shops like Valerie Confections and Le Pain du Jour ensure a particularly great start to any morning, along with freshly brewed coffee and even quiches. On the freshly prepared side, walking around quickly reveals pizza and pasta makers, simple breakfast operations and simple snacks like doughnuts, banh mi sandwiches, falafel and various Vietnamese dishes. Though many of the vendors change over time, there's always something great to enjoy.

And because of the market's longstanding positive relationship with not only the city of Santa Monica but also the restaurants and bars nearby, the weekly markets also pull in at least one big-name restaurant to prepare food on site each week. Local sushi spot Sugarfish is a recurring Wednesday add-on, as is the Border Grill gourmet food truck, which sells everything from tacos to tamales to delicious desserts. These change weekly and provide a great way for longtime market regulars to experience something new. Add in the coastline views and kind people and you've got perhaps the friendliest dining experience you can have outside of a restaurant.

LOS ANGELES STREET FOOD

HOLLYWOOD FARMERS MARKET

Open: 8:00 a.m. to 1:00 p.m. Sunday

Another longtime market operation is the Hollywood Farmers Market, located a block south of the storied Hollywood Walk of Fame and close to the iconic Sunset and Vine intersection.

Much like the Santa Monica Farmers Market, the Hollywood alternative draws a strong weekly crowd, though one with a decidedly smaller chef presence. Instead, the Sunday market in Hollywood is almost exclusively local, along with the occasional tourist presence (this is Hollywood, after all). That makes for a slightly quieter—though only a little less crowded—time, but one with all of the advantages of its Westside option.

Founded in 1991, the market spans the equivalent of several city blocks, except that it spreads out in all directions from a central intersection at Selma and Ivar Avenues. This forms the hub of the Hollywood Farmers Market itself, with vendors splaying out in tight clusters from there. There are usually less expensive vendors down toward Sunset, while the pricier real estate moves the opposite way toward Hollywood Boulevard. Fishmongers, bakers and preserve makers fan out toward the east, and most of the food on site moves west from the intersection, with a few different options available weekly.

Because the market is equally well known but less in demand, there's more stability at the Hollywood Farmers Market than in Santa Monica. Vendors stay longer, and it is easy for anyone who lives in the area to quickly establish a routine where they snack, shop and enjoy a leisurely Sunday in equal measure, every single week. However, it also means that there are fewer overall options here than in Santa Monica, but easier access and the same high quality means the balance of produce vendors to food vendors still works in your favor.

The real pro move at the Hollywood Farmers Market is to arrive early and immediately head for Bowers Gourmet Sausages for one of its secretly incredible breakfast burritos. Absolutely packed with everything from spinach to sausage to potatoes to cheese, each one is a mouthful unto itself and makes for more than enough to line your stomach while walking around.

Beyond that, the market is your oyster—no, really, you can enjoy plenty of freshly shucked oysters here. There are also vendors selling tamales, shawarma plates and kebabs, plus pupusas, Phily cheesesteaks, Thai food, crèpes and rotisserie chicken, to name a few. Don't forget dessert either, thanks to options as diverse as coconut cakes and snow cones. Talk about a great way to spend a Sunday.

THE STREET FOOD LANDSCAPE IN LOS ANGELES TODAY

YAMASHIRO FARMERS MARKET

Open: 5:00 p.m. to 9:00 p.m. on Thursdays during the summer only

For pure ambiance alone, there is absolutely no better farmers' market in Los Angeles than the one found high above Hollywood at Yamashiro (yes, that includes the ocean-adjacent Santa Monica Farmers Market). Hugging a hillside that offers unbridled views of all of Hollywood, as well as downtown and much of the South Bay when weather permits, the annual summertime market is less about the shopping as it is the experience.

In fact, it's entirely possible to have an amazing time at the Yamashiro Farmers Market and barely buy anything at all. It's all because of the seven-acre site itself, which sits on some of the most prime Hollywood Hills real estate you'll find. This was no fancy recent purchase, though; the Yamashiro site has existed intact for over one hundred years—a seemingly impossible feat in Los Angeles, which does not often share the rest of the world's penchant for holding on to old, beautiful things.

Yet that's exactly what the city has done with Yamashiro, which holds its namesake Yamashiro restaurant, as well as a poolside pagoda bar and several other outbuildings. The restaurant, which serves a unique take on Asian-influenced California cuisine, has for generations been a slightly hidden getaway for celebrities and locals alike. Done in a Japanese style, the beautiful wooden framework has been timeless since it was first created and serves as an incredible backdrop to a night out at the market.

Now, it's important to keep in mind that this isn't the sort of market for browsing, seeking out competing prices or really even haggling; the Yamashiro Farmers Market sits in one smallish section of the grounds at the top of the property and only contains anywhere from twelve to twenty total vendors. There are likely fewer than half a dozen fruit and vegetable stands, set up alongside a small range of cottage industry folks selling their homemade jams or jerkies and a smattering of other sellers. A small band plays, and there are some communal tables for relaxing, but that's about it.

Until, of course, you get to the food. Not only do standalone vendors make the trek up the hill for the Thursday night events, but Yamashiro executive chef Brock Kleweno himself operates a tent, usually selling his very wonderful brand of fusion tacos. For a time, Kleweno owned and operated a full restaurant down the hill, selling the tacos inside the massive Hollywood and Highland complex. Now, the only place to try them is at Yamashiro.

Ordering at Yuca's in Los Feliz. *Paul Bartunek.*

There's usually at least one vendor selling hot dogs and sausages, alongside someone working meat skewers and takoyaki. Crèpes are a common occurrence, as are pita sandwiches and snackier bites like candied apples and dried fruit. Popular food trucks also show up, like the ice cream sandwich artisans Coolhaus. Heirloom LA, a catering outfit with a knack for selling organic, high-quality entrees streetside, also routinely makes the rounds at the Yamashiro Farmers Market.

Best of all, you can actually drink on site. Beer, wine and cocktails are all available, both at the market itself and the nearby pagoda bar, which sits at the edge of a swimming pool and is absolutely unbeatable for relaxing and enjoying the view. The best view, in fact, of any farmers' market you'll find in town.

Sources

Arellano, Gustavo. *Taco USA: How Mexican Food Conquered America.* New York: Scribner, 2012.

Bhimji, Fazila. "Struggles, Urban Citizenship, and Belonging: The Experience of Undocumented Street Vendors and Food Truck Owners in Los Angeles." *Urban Anthropology and Studies of Cultural Systems and World Economic Development* 39, no. 4: 455–92.

Molina, Natalia. *Fit to be Citizens? Public Health and Race in Los Angeles, 1879–2939.* Los Angeles: University of California Press, 2006.

Index

INDEX

INDEX

INDEX

About the Author

Farley Elliott is a longtime food, drink and travel writer based in Los Angeles. A California transplant by way of northern New York, Farley quickly embraced Southern California's warm weather and incredible street food scene.

Farley spent the better part of his first four years in L.A. seeking out the best in street food, tacos, burgers and beer, keeping meticulous notes along the way. Eventually, he began writing weekly taco reviews for *Serious Eats* and burger rankings for *LAist*, before branching out into strip mall finds, restaurant news and larger print features for *LA Weekly*.

Currently, Farley is a senior editor at *Eater*, grabbing daily restaurant scoops, writing large-format trend pieces and highlighting the best that L.A.'s restaurant scene has to offer. He's also that guy from the "Tiny Hamsters Eating Tiny Burritos" Internet video. This is his first book.

Visit us at
www.historypress.net
....
This title is also available as an e-book